An American, a Mormon, and a Christian is a helpful resource for all who are seeking to understand the teachings of The Church of Jesus Christ of Latter-day Saints. Senator Hatch uses scripture, personal experience, and his testimony to present a clear and broad explanation of the gospel. As he teaches the principles, we glimpse the meaning and joy that those principles have brought to both his public and his private life, and we're reminded of the promise that each of us can feel that same joy.

—J. W. MARRIOTT JR.
Executive chairman and chairman of the
Board of Marriott International, Inc.

Senator Orrin Hatch brings to this project a lifetime of sincerely seeking to understand the doctrines of Christ and exemplifying them in his personal and professional life. This book is a masterful yet simple explanation of the restored gospel for those seeking truth and a powerful further witness to believers. Who better to write about this subject than Orrin Hatch, Utah's senior senator in Washington, DC? He honors his church covenants and his commitments to the people with equal integrity.

—JANICE KAPP PERRY
Latter-day Saint songwriter

This is a marvelous book written by an outstanding individual and a very influential senator—marvelous because it is clear, simple, and understandable and deals with the ultimate and eternal questions of life. Perfect for investigators and missionaries. Reinforcing and inspiring for anyone desiring a good basic understanding and compelling testimony of the magnificent work and wonder called "the Restoration."

—STEPHEN R. COVEY
Author of the international bestseller
The 7 Habits of Highly Effective People

AN AMERICAN

A MORMON AND

A CHRISTIAN

WHAT I BELIEVE

AN **AMERICAN**

A **MORMON** AND

A **CHRISTIAN**

WHAT I BELIEVE

SENATOR

ORRIN

HATCH

Foreword by JERRY BORROWMAN

PLAIN SIGHT PUBLISHING
AN IMPRINT OF CEDAR FORT, INC.
SPRINGVILLE, UTAH

ISBN 13: 978-1-4621-1159-6

Published by Plain Sight Publishing, an imprint of Cedar Fort, Inc.
2373 W. 700 S., Springville, UT 84663
Distributed by Cedar Fort, Inc., www.cedarfort.com

LIBRARY OF CONGRESS CATALOGING-IN-PUBLICATION DATA

Hatch, Orrin, 1934- author.
  [Higher laws]
  An American, a Mormon, and a Christian / Orrin G. Hatch.
    pages cm
  ISBN 13: 978-1-4621-1159-6
  Originally published in 1995 by Deseret Book Company under the title Higher laws.
  Includes bibliographical references and index.
  1. Church of Jesus Christ of Latter-day Saints--Doctrines. 2. Mormon Church. I. Title.

  BX8635.3.H38 2012
  230'.9332--dc23
                              2012018196

Cover design by Angela D. Olsen
Cover design © 2012 by Lyle Mortimer

Printed in the United States of America

10 9 8 7 6 5 4 3 2 1

CONTENTS

CONTENTS

PART 3: WHERE ARE WE GOING?

FOREWORD

ONE OF THE MOST intriguing aspects of the 2012 presidential election is the curiosity raised about candidate Mitt Romney's personal religion, most often called Mormonism. In talking with Senator Orrin Hatch about another project, I mentioned the fact that it's too bad that a well-known member of The Church of Jesus Christ of Latter-day Saints (the Mormons) hasn't written an easy-to-read book that explains the basic doctrines and practices of the LDS Church for those who are curious, as well as for those members who want an easy-to-use guide in talking about the Church with their family and friends. To this he replied, "I've done that." Surprised, I asked him to tell me more.

It turns out that Senator Hatch, who is well known for his love of country and his devotion to conservative principles, including the right to worship, has written a book that shares the fundamental beliefs of our church in a way that is of interest to fellow members and friends alike. I reviewed a copy and was intrigued at the excellence of the writing and encouraged him to publish it for the national public. What follows is the result of that effort.

Senator Orrin Hatch, the second longest serving Republican senator in U.S. history and a devoted member of The Church of Jesus Christ of Latter-day Saints, is undoubtedly known as a skilled orator and an effective legislator who has been a great spokesman for the conservative wing of the Republican Party for nearly four decades. He has also reached across the aisle to create meaningful laws and needed reform. He is one of the most effective senators in our history. But there's more to Orrin Hatch than his service in the United States Senate. He is a skilled writer and an extremely creative person who writes Grammy Award-winning music and lyrics. In this book, he does a masterful and concise job of teaching the basic beliefs of the Latter-day Saint Church. Because of the unique historical moment that exists at the time of this publication, he is one of the most recognizable members of the Mormon Church who is in a position to lay out its fundamental beliefs and doctrines for those who are curious and want to know more. With this book you can read a little to learn a lot.

One of the most puzzling things to members of our church is why some of our friends of other faiths insist on classifying us as "non-Christian." For example, Robert Jeffress, the senior pastor at First Baptist Church in Dallas, Texas, said of Romney, "Mitt Romney's a good moral person, but he's not a Christian. Mormonism is not Christianity. It has always been considered a cult by the mainstream of Christianity." That assertion is quite astonishing to most of my fellow Mormons. After all, we belong to The Church of Jesus Christ of Latter-day Saints, and the book we present to the world as a companion to the Holy Bible is The Book of Mormon, Another Testament of Jesus Christ.

In our church meetings we frequently cite the assertion by an ancient prophet that says, "We talk of Christ, we rejoice in Christ, we preach of Christ, we prophesy of Christ, and we write according to our prophecies, that our children may know to what source they may look for a remission of their sins." To us, it can't get any more Christian than that. Well, maybe it can.

Consider three of the first four of our thirteen articles of faith: 1) We believe in God, the Eternal Father, and in His Son, Jesus Christ, and in the Holy Ghost. 3) We believe that through the Atonement of Christ, all mankind may be saved, by obedience to the laws and ordinances of the Gospel. 4) We believe that the first principles and ordinances of the Gospel are: first, Faith in the Lord Jesus Christ; second, Repentance; third, Baptism by immersion for the remission of sins; fourth, Laying on of hands for the gift of the Holy Ghost.

These assertions of the divinity and Atonement of Jesus Christ are central to our worship and our daily lives. This is why fellow members in The Church of Jesus Christ of Latter-day Saints are hurt when others outside of our faith insist that we are not Christian. The reasons that leaders of other churches take issue with our doctrines are complex. Our beliefs about the beginning of life and the nature of the Godhood, along with our understanding of humankind's ultimate destiny, play into this incorrect notion. In this book, Senator Hatch lays out, in an easy-to-understand way, the basic beliefs and doctrines of the LDS Church as he understands them.

This is not an official publication of the Church. It is not Senator Hatch's mission to lay the many varied doctrines and understandings of other Christian denominations side-by-side with ours in comparison, since it is only fair that each of those churches explain their beliefs in their own way. Rather, Senator Hatch explains the reality of the living Christ and the central role He plays in our salvation. He speaks openly and candidly about our religious practices and how we implement them in our daily lives. He shares his personal testimony of why he believes these things to be true. In reading this book, you will come to understand Mormonism and why we take our faith so seriously.

One aspect of LDS doctrine that many people are unaware of is the unique sense of connection we feel to America and the ideals of the Founding Fathers. With over fourteen million members, we are the largest church in the world that was founded in America but based off the original church of Jesus Christ. We believe that this is a choice country that is blessed by God, that the Constitution of the United States was inspired by God, and that the freedom that America has inspired throughout the world makes us that "shining city on a hill" spoken of by Jesus in the New Testament.

From July 1846 through July 1847, the Mormon Battalion, the only religiously based unit in the history of the United States Army, marched under grueling conditions from Fort Leavenworth, Kansas, to San Diego, California, as part of the Mexican–American War that brought California and the vast territories of the West into the United States. This call to service for more than five hundred Mormon men couldn't have come at a worse time for the Church. The founder of the Church, Joseph Smith, Jr., had been murdered in Carthage, Illinois, three years earlier, and our members were being driven en masse to leave Illinois to cross the then uninhabitable Great Plains to settle in Salt Lake City, Utah. But, when their country called, newly appointed leader Brigham Young asked them to serve. And they did.

My grandfather, John Borrowman, was a member of the Battalion. After a march of more than twenty-five hundred miles through the great desert of the Southwest, it was the Mormons who helped lay claim to the great territories acquired from Mexico in that war, including Arizona, New Mexico, Colorado, Utah, and California. It was the Mormons who were working at Sutter's Mill when gold was discovered in 1849. So our history is much entwined with the history of this great country, and we take pride in having played a key role in establishing the United States as we know it today. Members of our church have served our country in every military conflict since then, and we have stepped up to leadership roles in Congress, government, education, and the arts and entertainment. We are your neighbors and hope to be your friends.

Now, because of this remarkable book by Senator Hatch, you can come to know what we believe and why we believe it. You already know how much he loves America. This book is an expression of his love of God. I hope you will read this with an open heart and mind.

—Jerry Borrowman
Award-winning author of military biography
and fiction, www.jerryborrowman.com

Jerry Borrowman and Rudi Wobbe are recipients of the National Award from the Freedoms Foundation at Valley Forge for "their contribution to freedom" for writing *Three against Hitler*. The first recipient of this prestigious award was President Dwight D. Eisenhower.

PREFACE

IN SALT LAKE CITY, on Temple Square, is a visitors' center with a beautiful oval staircase leading to an upper room. There the universe is depicted on a domed ceiling that hovers over a magnificent replica of Thorvaldson's sculpture of the Savior, *The Christus*.

Many visitors to Temple Square are amazed at the reverence Mormons have for Jesus Christ and at their overwhelming gratitude for his sacrifice. Some have been led to believe that Mormons are not Christians but rather are members of a sect not related to Christianity. To Mormons, this is astonishing and perplexing. From the Church's beginnings, the role of Jesus Christ has been central. The stated purpose of the Church is "to invite all to come unto Christ." Even the official name of the Church is The Church of Jesus Christ of Latter-day Saints. In fact, Mormons believe their religion to be a restoration (not a reformation) of the Church established anciently by the Savior himself. But because of controversy and considerable misinformation, many people believe that Mormons are not Christians, in spite of the fact that much readily available and easily understandable information explains otherwise.

Mormons are devout Christians who believe that Jesus Christ is the Son of God, who came to earth to atone for the sins of all people, so that through faith in him we might someday return to the presence of God. In fact we, as Mormons, believe in God the Eternal Father, in his Son Jesus Christ, and in the Holy Ghost—the Spirit sent from God to earth to testify of Christ.

THE BOOK OF MORMON: ANOTHER
TESTAMENT OF JESUS CHRIST

The term *Mormon* is a nickname derived from the Book of Mormon, a historical and religious account of early inhabitants of the Western Hemisphere. The Book of Mormon is one of the most widely disseminated books in history. It is available in every country and in almost every library. Its purpose, as stated on its title page, is "to the convincing of the Jew and Gentile that JESUS is the CHRIST, the ETERNAL GOD, manifesting himself unto all nations."

By reading the Book of Mormon, you will learn of prophets in the Western Hemisphere who knew of the mission of the Savior. They prophesied of Christ, ultimately knew the resurrected Christ, and promised you and me that if we will prayerfully read their record, having faith in Christ, he will manifest the truthfulness of it unto us by the power of the Holy Ghost. That is a magnificent promise!

The Book of Mormon is, as its subtitle proclaims, "Another Testament of Jesus Christ." Those who prayerfully read it can gain profound knowledge of the Son of God and his mission. The book is written to people of every faith. It is my hope that by reading it, you will come to understand why Mormons send more than 50,000 missionaries all over the world to tell about Christ and his gospel.

Latter-day Saints also believe in three other books of scripture: the Bible, the Doctrine and Covenants (a collection of revelations referred to in this book as the D&C), and the Pearl of Great Price (a collection of religious and historical records).

THE PURPOSE OF THIS BOOK

My own mother converted to Mormonism from Methodism many years ago. She passed away at eighty-nine years of age. After she read the manuscript for this book, Mom said, "Orrin, if only I'd had the benefit of this book when I was studying the gospel, I wouldn't have taken so much time to join the Church."

Mom was a great student of the scriptures. In addition, although she had no more than eight years of formal education, she was one of the brightest and most inquisitive people I have ever known. She was highly self-educated and, up to the day she died, she was a voracious reader of the scriptures. Her example is a principal reason I love the scriptures so much.

This book is not intended to be an exhaustive treatise on the gospel of Jesus Christ. Yet it discusses the most basic and important gospel principles. In these principles can be found the answers to three fundamental questions of life: Where did we come from? Why are we here? Where are we going? Those answers alone make this book worthwhile.

Many other important concepts are discussed, including the doctrine of the Godhead, the apostasy following the death of the Savior's apostles, the restoration of the gospel in our day, the true organization of Christ's church, why prophets are necessary today, the Book of Mormon, the first principles and ordinances of the gospel, what happens to those who have never heard the gospel while on the earth, and what happens to us and our families in the life hereafter. The answers to these questions and problems can play a significant role in strengthening our families, our communities, our country, and us.

I hope that as you read this book, you will do so humbly, praying for help from our Father in Heaven. If you will, I know he will help you understand these important doctrines and principles.

THE IMPORTANCE OF PERSONAL PRAYER

In the Hart Building in Washington, DC, every senator's office has a bathroom right off the private office. Mine has a little closet cubbyhole before the bathroom. Before I begin my work each day, I kneel in that closet and ask for God's help. I get to the office very early, because this time spent praying for extra help is extremely important to me. I seldom miss this opportunity to petition our Father in Heaven. When I fail to show this deference to God, usually because of tense pressures or meetings before I get to my private office, I don't seem to have the same blessings or results. I consider prayer one of the most important things I can do before beginning these stressful days as a senator.

Throughout each day, I find myself communicating with our Father in Heaven and thanking him for the help he always seems to give me when I am in tune with his Spirit. I also spend plenty of time asking him for help.

I am no better than anyone else. Like many in important positions, I know the value of prayer and reliance on a higher power. The good things that happen I always attribute to our Father in Heaven. And each night before retiring to bed, I kneel with my wife, Elaine. At the times when I feel the least close to God, I make it a point to stop and communicate with him.

The joy of understanding the doctrines explained in this brief book will be exciting to you. To ensure that you gain the fullest joy from it, please humble yourself; live Christ's teachings (see John 7:16–17); get on your knees and fervently pray to God for a witness that these scriptural doctrines are true. If you do these things, you will feel the influence of the Holy Ghost, and your spiritual eyes will see the deeper meanings of the doctrines discussed.

One of the exciting messages of this book is that God has raised up modern-day prophets to help us in this complex world. Harold B. Lee, one of these latter-day prophets, once said, "If you want the blessing, don't just kneel down and pray about it. Prepare yourselves in every conceivable way you can in order to make yourselves worthy to receive the blessings you seek" (*Stand Ye in Holy Places* [Salt Lake City: Deseret Book, 1975], 244).

Reading this book can prepare you to understand the Lord's work. As you read, pray constantly for help from God that the truth will be revealed to you.

Do not be afraid. God loves you. He listens to the prayers of every humble man, woman, and child.

How do you pray? There is no right or wrong way, but here are some guidelines that may be helpful.

We can learn a lot from our children. They are without guile. I remember one of my own children praying like this:

"Dear Heavenly Father. I love my mother and father. Thank you for them. Please bless them and me, in the name of Jesus, amen." In the child's own simple way, the basic steps for good prayer were outlined. Please allow me to make some suggestions so you will feel comfortable with your own prayers, both private and public.

Always address our Father in Heaven at the beginning of your prayer: "Our Father in Heaven," "Dear Heavenly Father," "Dear God," or something similar.

Take time to thank God for your blessings: "We thank thee."

God expects us to ask him for needed further blessings: "We ask thee."

End each prayer "In the name of Jesus Christ, amen."

In summary:

We address our Heavenly Father.

We thank him for our blessings.

We ask for blessings we need.

We end our prayer in the name of Christ.

It is that simple. Once you know these four simple steps, you can pray with confidence anytime, anywhere.

One further thing. It is good to use *thee*, *thou*, and similar language when speaking with our Father in Heaven. Doing so shows proper respect and reverence.

With these simple instructions, you are prepared to talk with your Father in Heaven. Do so. He won't let you down: "When thou prayest, enter into thy closet, and when thou hast shut thy door, pray to thy Father which is in secret; and thy Father which seeth in secret shall reward thee openly" (Matthew 6:6).

"As truly as I live, saith the Lord, as ye have spoken in mine ears, so will I do to you" (Numbers 14:28).

PART 1

WHERE DID WE COME FROM?

CHAPTER 1

OUR LIFE
BEFORE BIRTH

Our birth is but a sleep and a forgetting:
The soul that rises with us, our life's star,
Hath had elsewhere its setting,
And cometh from afar:
Not in entire forgetfulness,
And not in utter nakedness,
But trailing clouds of glory do we come
From God, who is our home.

—WORDSWORTH

MANY YEARS AGO, while serving a mission for my church, I met a wonderful woman in Ohio who had been diligently praying for answers to life's great questions. One day, while sitting in church, she saw a spiritual messenger who showed her two keys. One key was bronze and the other was silver. The messenger asked her which key she desired. She told him, "Silver, because it stands for redemption." The messenger looked pleased with her answer.

That evening she was sitting in her humble home, reading her church literature, when the same messenger appeared, this time with two coins. Again, one was bronze and the other was silver. When he asked which coin she would take, she gave the same answer. He again looked pleased, and he told her to "cling to the little black book" that would be given her, and she would find the answers to her prayers.

The very next day, my missionary companion and I knocked on her door, taught her a lesson on the gospel, and gave her a copy of the Book of Mormon, which at that time was bound in black.

That first day, she felt that she knew us, even though she had never met us before in this life. She was amazed at her feelings toward us, and when we taught her the gospel plan, she understood why.

How many times have we met people who we seem to know but can't remember having met them before? Isn't that a strange feeling? Probably all of us have had that experience. Why do we have it? I believe it is because we met them before we were born.

THE PREMORTAL EXISTENCE OF THE HUMAN RACE

Paul wrote to the Hebrews, "Both he that sanctifieth and they who are sanctified are all of one: for which cause he is not ashamed to call them brethren" (Hebrews 2:11). Jesus Christ, of course, is the one who sanctifies, and we who become Christians are the ones who are sanctified. Therefore, Christ is not ashamed to call us his brothers and sisters. But what is the "one" that we are all of? The New International Version of the Bible makes it clear: "Both the one who makes men holy and those who are made holy are of the *same family*." That is why Jesus calls us his brothers and sisters.

Revelation 3:14 calls Jesus "the faithful and true witness, *the beginning of the creation of God*." If he was the beginning of God's creation, then God must have created others after him.

Paul calls the Savior "the image of the invisible God, the *firstborn of every creature*" (Colossians 1:15). Paul also calls Jesus "the *firstborn among many brethren*" (Romans 8:29). If Jesus is the firstborn, others must have been born after him, his "brethren" (and sisters).

Since Jesus is the beginning of God's creation, the Firstborn among many brothers (and sisters), and since he identifies those brothers and sisters as us, we must conclude that we, too, are the children of our Heavenly Father.

The Bible teaches these truths in many other places. For example, when Mary went to embrace the Lord after his resurrection, he said to her, "Touch me not; for I am not yet ascended to my Father: but go to my brethren, and say unto them, I ascend unto my Father, and *your* Father; and to my God, and *your* God" (John 20:17). Similarly, the Savior began the Lord's Prayer with the words "*Our* Father which art in heaven" (Matthew 6:9).

Consider Numbers 16:22: "They fell upon their faces, and said, O God, *the God of the spirits of all flesh*, shall one man sin, and wilt thou be wroth with all the congregation?"

In John 3:13 the Savior taught, "No man hath ascended up to heaven, but he that came down from heaven, even the Son of man which is in heaven." The main point here is that Christ came down from heaven, but neither he nor any of us could return unless we first "came down from heaven." Therefore, we must have been in heaven with our spiritual Father, God, in a premortal existence.

An interesting extension of that argument is found in Ecclesiastes 12:7 (speaking of death): "Then shall the dust return to the earth as it was: and the spirit shall *return* unto God who gave it." How can we return to a place we have not been? Put another way, how could we return to the God who gave us life if we had not been with him before the world was created?

Paul wrote in Hebrews 12:9, "We have had fathers of our flesh which corrected us, and we gave them reverence: shall we not much rather be in subjection unto the Father of spirits, and live?" Surely God is the Father of our spirits.

Jeremiah wrote, "The word of the Lord came unto me, saying, *Before I formed thee in the belly I knew thee; and before thou camest forth out of the womb I sanctified thee, and I ordained thee a prophet unto the nations*" (Jeremiah 1:4–5). How much clearer could it be? How could Jeremiah have been known and preordained by God before his mother conceived him? If Jeremiah was ordained a prophet before the world was created, was he there alone, or were we there with him?

On one occasion, Jesus "saw a man which was *blind from his birth*. And his disciples asked him, saying, Master, who did sin, this man, or his parents, that he was born blind? Jesus answered, Neither hath this man sinned, nor his parents: but that the works of God should be made manifest in him" (John 9:1–3). When could the man have sinned if he was "blind from his birth?" The disciples knew of the premortal, spiritual existence where he might have sinned. Otherwise, they would not have asked that question.

Paul, on Mars Hill, preached to the men of Athens who worshiped at a statue dedicated to the "unknown god." He told them that they were superstitious and that he would tell them about the real God: "Whom . . . ye ignorantly worship, him declare I unto you" (Acts 17:23). Paul did so, ending his discourse with these words: "As certain . . . of your own poets have said, *For **we are also his offspring**. Forasmuch then as **we are the offspring of God**, we ought not to think that the Godhead is like unto gold, or silver, or stone, graven by art and man's device*" (verses 28–29).

We can also learn much from the penetrating questions God asked his servant Job: "*Where wast thou when I laid the foundations of the earth*? declare, if thou hast understanding. Who hath laid the measures thereof, if thou knowest? or who hath stretched the line upon it? Whereupon are the foundations thereof fastened? or who laid the corner stone thereof; *when the morning stars sang together, and all the sons of God shouted for joy*?" (Job 38:4–7)

Have we met before? I believe we have. Where did we come from? We came from God. We lived with him as brothers and sisters before we were born into this mortal existence. Jesus Christ is our Elder Brother. Our Heavenly Father loves us and cares about us. He cares about you. You are one of his children.

CHAPTER 2

THE GODHEAD

The earth, the sun and stars, and the universe itself, and the charming variety of the seasons, demonstrate the existence of a Divinity.

—PLATO

If God did not exist, it would be necessary to invent Him.

—VOLTAIRE

WHAT DO WE KNOW about the Father of our spirits, about our Father in Heaven? What can we learn about him from the scriptures? Jesus himself prayed to the Father, "This is life eternal, that they might know thee the only true God, and Jesus Christ, whom thou hast sent" (John 17:3). If our eternal life depends on knowing the truth about God, then we must begin searching for that truth.

THE ATHANASIAN CREED

Within a few centuries after Jesus and his apostles had left the earth, the Council of Nicea, in AD 325, promulgated the Nicene Creed, which was soon followed by the Athanasian Creed: "We worship one God in Trinity, and Trinity in Unity, neither confounding the persons, nor dividing the substance. For there is one

7

person of the Father, another of the Son, and another of the Holy Ghost. But the Godhead of the Father, Son, and Holy Ghost, is all one; the glory equal, the majesty coeternal. Such as the Father is, such is the Son, and such is the Holy Ghost. The Father uncreate, the Son uncreate, and the Holy Ghost uncreate. The Father incomprehensible, the Son incomprehensible, and the Holy Ghost incomprehensible. The Father eternal, the Son eternal, and the Holy Ghost eternal. And yet there are not three eternals, but one eternal. As also there are not three incomprehensibles, nor three uncreated; but one uncreated and one incomprehensible. So likewise the Father is Almighty, the Son Almighty, and the Holy Ghost Almighty; and yet there are not three Almighties, but one Almighty. So the Father is God, the Son is God, and the Holy Ghost is God, and yet there are not three Gods but one God."

In my humble opinion, this statement is a mass of inconsistencies and contradictions that has little to do with what the scriptures say God is like. We cannot understand God, our Eternal Father, unless we embrace his words in the scriptures. No other source, including the debated concepts of the Council of Nicea, is adequate.

Some churches teach that the Father, Son, and Holy Ghost are one being, essence, or substance, like water, steam, and ice—three different aspects of the same thing. They also teach that God is a spirit without body, parts, or passions. Are these teachings biblically correct? No!

THE FATHER, SON, AND HOLY GHOST
ARE THREE SEPARATE BEINGS

Stephen, the first Christian martyr, having told the Jews they had crucified their Messiah, was stoned to death. However, before he died, he had a marvelous vision: "He, being full of the Holy Ghost, looked up steadfastly into heaven, and saw the glory of God, and Jesus standing on the right hand of God, and said, Behold, I see the heavens opened, and the Son of man standing on the right hand of God" (Acts 7:55–56).

How clear the scriptures are! Stephen saw God the Father and Jesus standing at his Father's right hand. In addition, Stephen was filled with the Holy Ghost so he could see spiritually. This scripture flies in the face of the Athanasian Creed, showing three distinct beings in the Godhead. Several other scriptures prove this as well.

Matthew 3:16–17, for example, describes the Savior's baptism: "Jesus, when he was baptized, went up straightway out of the water: and, lo, the heavens were opened unto him, and he saw the Spirit of God descending like a dove, and lighting upon him: And lo a voice from heaven, saying, This is my beloved Son, in whom I am well pleased." Here again, the Bible mentions three separate beings— God the Father, Jesus the Son, and the Holy Ghost.

Jesus also spoke some profound truths to Mary: "Touch me not; for I am not yet ascended to my Father: but go to my brethren, and say unto them, I ascend unto my Father, and your Father; and to my God, and your God" (John 20:17). Here Jesus refers to his Father as our Father and his God as our God, clearly delineating the separate status and function of God the Eternal Father and Jesus Christ his Son.

In Hebrews 1:1–3 we read: "God . . . hath in these last days spoken unto us by his Son, whom he hath appointed heir of all things, by whom also he made the worlds; who being the brightness of his glory, and the express image of his person, and upholding all things by the word of his power, when he had by himself purged our sins, sat down on the right hand of the Majesty on high." Christ was the heir of all things, made the worlds under the Father's direction, spoke to us at the direction of the Father, and was in the express image of God. Clearly, the Father and the Son are two separate and distinct beings with different missions and functions.

In John 14:16–17, Christ speaks of the Holy Ghost: "I will pray the Father, and he shall give you another Comforter, that he may abide with you for ever; even the Spirit of truth; whom the world cannot receive, because it seeth him not, neither knoweth him: but ye know him; for he dwelleth with you, and shall be in you."

Christ identifies this "Comforter" in John 14:26, just a few verses later: "The Comforter, *which is the Holy Ghost, whom the Father will send in my name,* he shall teach you all things, and bring all things to your remembrance, whatsoever I have said unto you."

Clearly, the Comforter, or the Holy Ghost, is a spirit sent from God to earth to comfort us after Christ left the earth. He is the "Spirit of truth," will "teach" us all things, and will "bring all things" that Christ said to our remembrance.

In John 16:13–14 we read: "When he, the Spirit of truth, is come, he will guide you into all truth: *for he shall not speak of himself;* but whatsoever he shall hear, that shall he speak: and he will shew you things to come. *He shall glorify me*: for he shall receive of mine, and shall shew it unto you."

In John 16:7–8 Jesus said, "It is expedient for you that I go away: for if I go not away, the Comforter will not come unto you; but if I depart, I will send him unto you. And when he is come, he will reprove the world of sin, and of righteousness, and of judgment."

There actually is a Father, a Son, and a Holy Ghost—three separate and distinct beings, each with a different mission and function.

GOD AND CHRIST HAVE PERFECT BODIES OF FLESH AND BONES

Most churches teach that God is a spirit without a body. However, a number of scriptures disprove that idea.

Genesis 1:26–27: "God said, Let us make man in our image, after our likeness: and let them have dominion over the fish of the sea, and over the fowl of the air, and over the cattle, and over all the earth, and over every creeping thing that creepeth upon the earth. So God created man in his own image, in the image of God created he him; male and female created he them." Every person is born with a body of flesh and bones. And since we are created in the image of God, God also must have a body of flesh and bones.

Some argue that these verses refer to our spiritual bodies and not our physical bodies. However, look at Genesis 5:1–3: "This is the book of the generations of Adam. In the day that God created man, in the likeness of God made he him; male and female created he them; and blessed them, and called their name Adam, in the day when they were created. And Adam lived an hundred and thirty years, *and begat a son in his own likeness, after his image; and called his name Seth.*"

Seth, of course, had a body of flesh and bones as well as a spirit, yet he was begotten in the image and likeness of his father, Adam, who also had a body of flesh and bones and a spirit and who was created in the image and likeness of God. Therefore, God must be a tangible being with a perfect body of flesh and bones as well as a spirit.

Look at Genesis 32:30, which gives the words of the Prophet Jacob: "I have seen God *face to face*, and my life is preserved."

Exodus 24:9–10 says: "Then went up Moses, and Aaron, Nadab, and Abihu, and seventy of the elders of Israel: and they saw the God of Israel: and there was *under his feet* as it were a paved work of a sapphire stone, and as it were the body of heaven in his clearness. And upon the nobles of the children of Israel he *laid not his hand*: also they saw God, and did eat and drink."

Exodus 33:9–11 is quite explicit: "As Moses entered into the tabernacle, the cloudy pillar descended, and stood at the door of the tabernacle, and the Lord talked with Moses. And all the people saw the cloudy pillar stand at the tabernacle door: and all the people rose up and worshiped, every man in his tent door. *And the Lord spake unto Moses face to face, as a man speaketh unto his friend.*"

On the cross, the Savior said, "Father, into thy hands I commend my spirit" (Luke 23:46). Then he died. What was it that left his body? It was his spirit. James 2:26 tells us this is what death is—the separation of the body and the spirit: "*The body without the spirit is dead.*" Yet three days later, Christ's spirit came back into his body, and he became a resurrected being.

Later, Christ appeared to his apostles in the upper room: "Jesus himself stood in the midst of them, and saith unto them, Peace be unto you. But they were terrified and affrighted, and supposed that they had seen a spirit. And he said unto them, Why are ye troubled? and why do thoughts arise in your hearts? Behold my hands and my feet, that it is I myself: handle me, and see; *for a spirit hath not flesh and bones, as ye see me have*" (Luke 24:36–39).

Even though the apostles thought him to be only a spirit, Christ as a resurrected being showed them that his spirit had reunited with his body of flesh and bones.

Would Christ ever die again? What is death? According to the scriptures, death is the separation of the spirit from the body.

Romans 6:9 is relevant: "Christ being raised from the dead dieth no more; death hath no more dominion over him." In other words, Christ would never die again. That means his spirit would never again leave his resurrected, perfect body of flesh and bones.

Philippians 3:20–21 makes sense of the resurrection: "Our conversation is in heaven; from whence also we look for the Saviour, the Lord Jesus Christ: *Who shall change our vile body, that it may be fashioned like unto his glorious body,* according to the working whereby he is able even to subdue all things unto himself."

Paul in that verse describes a perfect resurrected body that would have power even over the physical elements. Thus, it is easier to understand how Christ could have suddenly appeared to the apostles in the upper room.

If Christ, as a resurrected being—with his spirit in a perfect body of flesh and bones—is in the express image of God the Father, then what kind of being must the Father be? He also must be a perfect being, a spirit clothed with a perfect body of flesh and bones.

This analysis gives even greater meaning to these scriptures:

1 Corinthians 3:16–17 talks about the importance of our bodies: "Know ye not that ye are the temple of God, and that the Spirit of God dwelleth in you? If any man defile the temple of God, him shall God destroy; for the temple of God is holy, which temple ye are."

We are brought here to earth, outside the presence of God, to gain an earthly body in form similar to his. However, our bodies are mortal and will remain so until the resurrection, when they will be changed to be like his "glorious body . . . whereby he is able even to subdue all things unto himself" (Philippians 3:21).

James 3:8–9 reveals that we are created in the similitude of God: "The tongue can no man tame; it is an unruly evil, full of deadly poison. Therewith bless we God, even the Father; and therewith curse we men, which are made after the similitude of God."

Again, the fact that we are made after the similitude of God lends great weight to the above arguments. These teachings also help us to better understand God. We can now visualize him as a supreme heavenly being who is perfect and is a real Father in Heaven.

Arguing that God does not have a body, some people cite John 4:24: "God is a Spirit: and they that worship him must worship him in spirit and in truth." Of course God is a spirit. *All* of us are spirits, but we are clothed with bodies of flesh and bones.

So is God. So is the resurrected Christ.

Again consider John 4:24, but every time you see the word "spirit" insert "without a body": "*God is a Spirit* (without a body): *and they that worship him must worship him in spirit* (without a body) *and in truth.*" This passage becomes confusing if read in this manner. But turn it around and put "with a body" after the word "spirit": "*God is a Spirit,* with a body: *and they that worship him must worship him in spirit,* with a body, *and in truth.*"

Now the verse makes sense. If God were only a spirit, if we wanted to worship him in spirit, we would have to hang up our bodies outside the church house so we could go in and "worship him in spirit."

Some cite John 17:20–22 to show that the Father, Son, and Holy Ghost are one being. Christ was in the Garden of Gethsemane, praying for the eleven apostles (Judas had left to betray him). There Christ said, "Neither pray I for these alone, but for them also which shall believe on me through their word; that they all may be one; as thou, Father, art in me, and I in thee, that they also may be one in us: that the world may believe that thou hast sent me. And the glory which thou gavest me I have given them; that they may be one, even as we are one."

Some use these verses to argue that the Father, Son, and Holy Ghost are one being and not three separate beings. But remember that Christ was praying not only for "these alone," meaning the apostles, but "for them also which shall believe on me through their word." That includes you, me, and every other person who believes in the New Testament: "That they all may be one; as thou, Father, art in me, and I in thee, that they also may be one in us." Clearly, Christ wanted the apostles, you and me, and every other Christian to be one as he and his Father are one. Did he mean one big, amorphous being with arms and legs sticking out all over? The image is interesting but incorrect. He wanted us to be one in purpose, faith, and works, as he and his Father are.

The same concept applies to John 10:30: "I and my Father are one." "One" means unified in purpose, faith, dedication, and action.

God is a being of body, parts, and passions.

God has a face, for in Exodus 33:11, he spoke to Moses face to face.

God has a voice, for his voice was heard by Adam and Eve (Genesis 3:8); by Cain (Genesis 4:9); by Moses, Aaron, and Miriam (Numbers 12:4); and by the Israelites as a body (Deuteronomy 5:22).

God is a jealous God (Exodus 20:5; 34:14; Deuteronomy 6:15).

God can show anger (Deuteronomy 6:15; Judges 2:14; 3:8; 1 Kings 13:3–5; Isaiah 30:27).

God can be provoked to anger (Jeremiah 7:19–20; 1 Kings 22:53).

God has wrath against unrighteousness (Romans 1:18; Revelation 15:1, 7).

God is merciful and shows mercy (Exodus 20:6; 34:6, 7; Deuteronomy 4:31; 7:9).

In Nehemiah 9:17, God is described as gracious, merciful, slow to anger, and kind. (See also Psalm 116:5; James 5:11.)

God is literally our spiritual Father. Through his Son, he created this earth so we could come here, outside his presence, to be tested, make our own choices, and ultimately, upon conditions of righteousness, return to his presence as resurrected beings. (See 1 Corinthians 15:20–22.)

CHAPTER 3

THE ANTIQUITY
OF THE GOSPEL

The scripture, foreseeing that God would justify the heathen through faith, preached before the gospel unto Abraham, saying, In thee shall all nations be blessed.

—GALATIANS 3:8

I ONCE MET a highly educated person who claimed to be agnostic. He said that Christ was a plagiarist because he had borrowed philosophical and moral thoughts from other religions or philosophical systems. He cited the Dead Sea Scrolls as evidence that baptisms were performed before the time of Christ. In addition, he referred to early Buddhist teachings as further evidence that Christ stole his ideas from the past.

The Old Testament chronicles the time from the Creation until approximately 400 BC. Many Christians love the Old Testament yet feel that the New Testament is the only doctrinal guide necessary for their salvation. Many feel that Christianity began in AD 30 when Christ started his ministry in the Holy Land. But what kind of a God would have left generations without any knowledge of his gospel or of his Son, the premortal Jehovah of the Old Testament, the Jesus Christ of the New Testament?

Most Christians believe that the gospel did not reach the earth until Christ brought it during his ministry in the meridian of time (AD 30–34). As a result, some have been troubled by the arguments of agnostics who claim that some of the greatest philosophical tenets articulated by Christ and adopted by Christianity were taught on the earth before the advent of Jesus. For instance, the Buddhists taught a golden rule, "Do as ye would be done by," approximately seven hundred years before Christ came to earth. Did Christ borrow that from the Buddhists?

The Dead Sea Scrolls, written by the Essenes, who predated Christ, show that the Essenes practiced baptism similar to the one John the Baptist practiced when he baptized Jesus. The Essenes also practiced other Christian tenets long before Christ came to the earth.

Consequently, some agnostic critics have accused Christ of plagiarism. Was Christ a plagiarist? Not according to the New Testament. The New Testament confirms that the gospel has been on the earth from the beginning.

THE GOSPEL WAS PREACHED ANCIENTLY

In Galatians 3:8, speaking about father Abraham in the Old Testament, Paul says, "The scripture, foreseeing that God would justify the heathen through faith, preached before the gospel unto Abraham, saying, In thee shall all nations be blessed." In other words, Abraham knew of the gospel centuries before Christ came to the earth.

In Hebrews 11:24–26 we learn, "By faith Moses, when he was come to years, refused to be called the son of Pharaoh's daughter; choosing rather to suffer affliction with the people of God, than to enjoy the pleasures of sin for a season; esteeming the *reproach of Christ* greater riches than the treasures in Egypt: for he had respect unto the recompense of the reward."

Paul tells us that Moses esteemed the "reproach of Christ" centuries before Christ ever came to the earth. The "reproach of Christ" was Christ's gospel.

Consider 1 Corinthians 10:1–4: "I would not that ye should be ignorant, how that all our fathers were under the cloud, and all passed through the sea; and were all baptized unto Moses in the cloud and in the sea; and did all eat the same spiritual meat; and did all drink the same spiritual drink: for they drank of that spiritual Rock that followed them: *and that rock was Christ*." What were the "spiritual meat" and "spiritual drink" spoken of in these verses? These metaphors refer to the gospel of Jesus Christ. If Moses and the Israelites ate the spiritual meat and drank the spiritual drink, they must have known the gospel many centuries before Christ came to earth. These early prophets were taught the gospel through revelation from Jehovah, much as Christ taught the apostles the gospel during his mortal ministry.

In Hebrews 4:2, Paul continues his explanation that the gospel was preached to Moses and the Israelites many centuries before Christ: "Unto us was *the gospel* preached, as well as unto them: but the word preached did not profit them, not being mixed with faith in them that heard it."

Yes, the gospel was preached to the people at the time of Moses. But they didn't accept it or profit from it, as they should have. Christ's gospel has been on the earth from the beginning. As explained in the next chapter, he was Jehovah of the Old Testament, and he did speak to the people of that age. He did not leave them without his teachings. Christ was not a plagiarist.

A verse in the Book of Mormon explains these biblical scriptures and enlightens us about the antiquity of the gospel. The Book of Mormon prophet Alma, seventy-six years before the birth of Christ, said, "The Lord doth grant unto all nations, of their own nation and tongue, to teach his word, yea, in wisdom, all that he seeth fit that they should have; therefore we see that the Lord doth counsel in wisdom, according to that which is just and true" (Alma 29:8).

Alma makes clear that the Lord may have given some of his gospel to many nations. If that is so, the Buddhists could have borrowed from Christ's teachings.

All these scriptures explain that Christ was not a plagiarist but rather was the one who revealed the gospel from the beginning. Some of the other nations may have aspects of the gospel in their traditions, writings, and beliefs. Perhaps this explains some of the philosophical similarities between Christianity and other religions.

Perhaps if we had all the missing books of scripture mentioned in the Bible, we would have a greater awareness of the spreading of the gospel of Christ from the beginning. There are many scriptures that refer to books of the Bible that have been lost over the years.

(See Exodus 24:7; Numbers 21:14; Joshua 10:13; 1 Samuel 10:25; 1 Kings 11:41; 1 Chronicles 29:29; 2 Chronicles 9:29; 12:15; 20:34; 26:21; 33:19; 1 Corinthians 5:9; Ephesians 3:3; Colossians 4:16; and Jude 1:3, 14.)

CHAPTER 4

CHRIST AND THE OLD TESTAMENT

Other books were given for our information. The Bible was given for our transformation.

—ANONYMOUS

M Y MOTHER CONSTANTLY taught me Bible stories out of the Old Testament. I will forever be grateful for our times together, for her counsel, instructions, and testimony of the truthfulness of the Bible. I was twenty years old when I first read the Old Testament from the beginning to the end. Numbers and Leviticus were difficult, but the rest of the Old Testament had a profound impact on me, not only through its beautiful, exemplary stories, but also through the doctrines and moral teachings it so elegantly conveys.

As I grew older and had the opportunity to become a more serious student of the Old Testament, I began to realize how profound it is. It is the premier presage for the coming of Christ in the meridian of time and for his later second coming in what Paul referred to as the dispensation of the fulness of times (Ephesians 1:9–10).

Many people don't realize that references to Christ and his teachings are found throughout the Old Testament. Christ said in the New Testament, "Search the scriptures; for in them ye think ye have eternal life: *and they are they which testify of me*" (John 5:39). To what was he referring? The New Testament had not yet been written, so the scriptures to which he referred had to be the Old Testament.

Christ made it abundantly clear how important the Old Testament is in testifying of him.

CHRIST IS JEHOVAH

In fact, the Jehovah of the Old Testament is our Savior, the Jesus Christ of the New Testament. This can clearly be seen by comparing these verses from the Old and New Testaments. Old Testament passages are on the left; New Testament, on the right.

In Psalm 22:16–18, Jehovah prophesied the Crucifixion. Compare Matthew 27:35, which describes the death of Jesus.

"Dogs have compassed me: the assembly of the wicked have inclosed me: they pierced my hands and my feet. I may tell all my bones: they look and stare upon me. They part my garments among them, and cast lots upon my vesture."	"They crucified him, and parted his garments, casting lots: that it might be fulfilled which was spoken by the prophet, They parted my garments among them, and upon my vesture did they cast lots." (See also Mark 15:24; Luke 23:33; John 19:23.)

In Zechariah 12:10, Jehovah again prophesied the crucifixion. Compare John 19:34–37, where the prophecy is fulfilled.

"I will pour upon the house of David, and upon the inhabitants of Jerusalem, the spirit of grace and of supplications: and *they shall look upon me whom they have pierced.*"	"One of the soldiers with a spear pierced his side . . . that the scripture should be fulfilled . . . *They shall look on him whom they pierced.*"

In Exodus 3:13–14, Jehovah identified himself as "I AM." In John 8:58, Jesus used the same words to refer to himself.

"I AM THAT I AM: . . . Thus shalt thou say unto the children of Israel, I AM hath sent me unto you."	"Jesus said unto them, Verily, verily, I say unto you, Before Abraham was, I am."

In Psalm 41:9 Jehovah prophesied betrayal. In Acts 1:16–18, Paul explained the treachery of Judas.

"Mine own familiar friend, in whom I trusted, which did eat of my bread, hath lifted up his heel against me."

"Men and brethren, this scripture must needs have been fulfilled, which the Holy Ghost by the mouth of David spake before concerning Judas, which was guide to them that took Jesus. For he was numbered with us, and had obtained part of this ministry. Now this man purchased a field with the reward of iniquity; and falling headlong, he burst asunder in the midst, and all his bowels gushed out."

In Isaiah 12:2, Isaiah called Jehovah "my salvation." In Acts 4:12, Paul explained the source of salvation. He was clearly speaking about Jesus of Nazareth (see verse 10):

"God is my salvation; I will trust, and not be afraid: for the Lord JEHOVAH is my strength and my song; he also is become my salvation."

"Neither is there salvation in any other: for there is none other name under heaven given among men, whereby we must be saved."

In Isaiah 45:23, Jehovah explains that all will give him allegiance. Paul wrote in Philippians 2:10–11 that all would acknowledge Jesus as the Savior.

"I have sworn by myself, the word is gone out of my mouth in righteousness, and shall not return, That unto me every knee shall bow, every tongue shall swear."

"At the name of Jesus every knee should bow, of things in heaven, and things in earth; and things under the earth: and . . . every tongue . . . confess that Jesus Christ is Lord."

In Deuteronomy 32:3–4, Jehovah is described. Then in 1 Corinthians 10:1–4, Paul makes clear that the Rock mentioned in Deuteronomy is Christ.

"I will publish the name of the Lord: ascribe ye greatness unto our God. He is the Rock, his work is perfect: for all his ways are judgment: a God of truth and without iniquity, just and right is he."

"[The children of Israel] drank of that spiritual Rock that followed them: and that Rock was Christ."

Note also Isaiah 26:19: "Thy dead men shall live, together with my dead body shall they arise." Is Jehovah not speaking here of his future resurrection as Jesus the Christ?

I have selected only a few scriptures on this subject, but clearly the Jehovah of the Old Testament was none other than the premortal Jesus Christ.

PART 2

WHY ARE
WE HERE?

CHAPTER 5

THE FALL AND
THE ATONEMENT

Adam ate the apple, and our teeth still ache.

—Hungarian Proverb

Whosoever shall call on the name of the Lord shall be saved.

—Acts 2:21

WHY WAS THE GOSPEL preached from the beginning? Why was it necessary for the Savior to come? Because we are born into a fallen world—the result of the transgression of Adam and Eve.

Many churches teach that Adam brought sin into the world by committing sexual transgression with Eve in the Garden of Eden. They say that brought us all into this world as "born in sin." Nothing could be farther from the truth.

In fact, Adam and Eve, our first parents, furthered the work of God in providing the means for us to have our experience in mortality. The teachings of the churches of today arise from a misunderstanding of the scriptures.

THE TRUE NATURE OF THE FALL

If Adam had not fallen, he and Eve would have remained in a state of innocence and could not have had children while in the

Garden of Eden. The Book of Mormon is especially helpful in explaining this.

In 2 Nephi 2:22–23, the Book of Mormon prophet Lehi speaks of Adam and Eve's premortal state: "If Adam had not transgressed he would not have fallen, but he would have remained in the garden of Eden. And all things which were created must have remained in the same state in which they were after they were created; and they must have remained forever, and had no end. And they would have had no children; wherefore they would have remained in a state of innocence, having no joy, for they knew no misery; doing no good, for they knew no sin."

One of the great latter-day apostles, James E. Talmage, in his seminal work *Jesus the Christ*, wrote, "The fall was a natural process, resulting through the incorporation into the bodies of our first parents of the things that came from food unfit, through the violation of the command of God regarding what they should eat. Don't go around whispering that the fall consisted in the mother of the race losing her chastity and her virtue. It is not true; the human race is not born of fornication" ([Salt Lake City: Deseret Book, 1915], 30).

ADAM AND EVE WERE GIVEN TWO COMMANDMENTS BY GOD:

1. Multiply and replenish the earth (Genesis 1:28)
2. Do not partake of the forbidden fruit (Genesis 2:17)

These commandments were mutually exclusive. To keep one, they had to break the other. To multiply and replenish the earth, they had to partake of the forbidden fruit. That brought about a transformation in their bodies. It changed them from immortal but imperfect beings to mortal beings capable of conceiving children.

According to Talmage, the fall occurred because Adam and Eve ate food that was unfit for their immortal bodies (the forbidden fruit), which brought about a change that made them mortal and thus subject to death. Remember, we shouted for joy in the premortal existence at the possibility of coming to earth, obtaining a body, and becoming more like our Father in Heaven (Job 38:4–7). Adam and Eve had to partake of the forbidden fruit for these things to happen.

They are our first parents and have provided us the means of coming to earth to "work out our own salvation with fear and trembling" (Philippians 2:12).

The human race was not born of fornication. Adam and Eve were not immoral. United in marriage by God, this noble couple chose to bring us into the world. Now, outside the presence of God, we have the opportunity to choose for ourselves whether or not to live God's teachings.

Adam made a conscious choice to be the father of the human race. Adam was not deceived. Satan beguiled Eve (1 Timothy 2:14). Nevertheless, Eve did a good thing in partaking of the forbidden fruit. Who can criticize our first mother and father for providing us the opportunity to come into this world?

As a result of Adam and Eve's transgression and the resultant "fall," physical death came upon all people. And, in the sense that we are moved outside the presence of our Father in Heaven (Adam and Eve were banished from the Garden of Eden), spiritual death, or banishment from the presence of God, was the result.

Therefore we needed a Savior to atone for our sins, bring about the resurrection, and return us to the presence of God. Christ's sacrifice made it possible for us to overcome death of both body and spirit. Because of this sacrifice, or atonement, we can repent, be forgiven, be strengthened by the Holy Ghost, be spiritually healed, and find peace.

THE ATONEMENT OF JESUS CHRIST

Christ's sacrifice was voluntary. He said, "My Father love[s] me, because I lay down my life, that I might take it again. No man taketh it from me, but I lay it down of myself. I have power to lay it down, and I have power to take it again. This commandment have I received of my Father" (John 10:17–18).

Again in Matthew 26:53, Christ reaffirmed his power: "Thinkest thou that I cannot now pray to my Father, and he shall presently give me more than twelve legions of angels?"

In Hebrews 1:1–3 Paul tells us, "God, who at sundry times and in divers manners spake in time past unto the fathers by the prophets, hath in these last days spoken unto us by his Son, whom he hath appointed heir of all things, by whom also he made the worlds; who being the brightness of his glory, and the express image of his person, and upholding all things by the word of his power, when *he had by himself purged our sins,* sat down on the right hand of the Majesty on high." Christ's atoning sacrifice can purge us of our sins.

In Hebrews 2:9 Paul says, "Jesus . . . *was made a little lower than the angels* for the suffering of death, crowned with glory and honour; *that he by the grace of God should taste death for every man.*"

In Hebrews 5:9, Christ is called the "author of eternal salvation unto all them that obey him."

In 1 Peter 1:18–20, the Atonement is described in the following words: "Ye were not redeemed with corruptible things, as silver and gold, from your vain conversation received by tradition from your fathers; *but with the precious blood of Christ, as of a lamb without blemish and without spot*: who verily was foreordained before the foundation of the world, but was manifest in these last times for you."

Leviticus 17:11 explains that the sacrificial death of Christ was prefigured by the altar sacrifices under the law of Moses of the Old Testament.

The quintessential illustration of the expected atoning sacrifice of the Father and the Son is in Genesis 22. Abraham was told by the Lord, "Take now thy son, thine only son Isaac, whom thou lovest, and get thee into the land of Moriah; and offer him there for a burnt offering upon one of the mountains which I will tell thee of" (Genesis 22:2). Abraham, with perfect faith, took his only son, Isaac, "stretched forth his hand, and took the knife to slay his son. And the angel of the Lord called unto him out of heaven, and said, Abraham, Abraham: and he said, Here am I. And he said, Lay not thine hand upon the lad, neither do thou any thing unto him: for now I know that thou fearest God, seeing thou hast not withheld thy son, thine only son from me" (Genesis 22:10–12).

This was a representation or type of the sacrifice provided by our Father in Heaven. He gave his only begotten son as a sacrifice for all of us—yes, the lamb without blemish and without spot; the firstling of the flock (1 Peter 1:19–20).

I have always wondered how Abraham could have tolerated even contemplating sacrificing his son. One of the reasons he was commanded to leave Ur of the Chaldees was because the people of that area were practicing human sacrifice. How could he have proceeded to sacrifice his son without protesting to God about this command? This seemingly blind obedience has bothered many students of the scriptures. But the following scriptures give us explanations.

In James 2:21–23, James asked, "Was not Abraham our father justified by works, when he had offered Isaac his son upon the altar? Seest thou how faith wrought with his works, and by works was faith made perfect? And the scripture was fulfilled which saith, Abraham believed God, and it was imputed unto him for righteousness: and he was called the Friend of God." So, Abraham, as a prophet of God, had implicit faith in God and in God's commandments to him.

In Hebrews 11:17–19, a grand explanation is given: "By faith Abraham, when he was tried, offered up Isaac: and he that had received the promises offered up his only begotten son, of whom it was said, That in Isaac shall thy seed be called: Accounting that God *was able to raise him up, even from the dead*; from whence also he received him in a figure."

Abraham's faith was called perfect because he believed that God would raise Isaac up even if he had to sacrifice Isaac as a burnt offering on Moriah. Abraham, in his faithful, innocent understanding of Christ's foreordained work, knew there would be a resurrection. He knew that God would not abandon him. Yet, the analogy between Isaac, the only begotten son of Abraham and Sarah, and Christ, the only begotten Son of God in the flesh, was dramatic and a type or symbol for the ages.

In John 3:16–17, John shows the importance of God's love for us: "God so loved the world, that he gave his only begotten Son, that whosoever believeth in him should not perish, but have everlasting life. For God sent not his Son into the world to condemn the world; but that the world through him might be saved."

In 1 John 4:9, again God's love is expressed: "In this was manifested the love of God toward us, because that God sent his only begotten Son into the world, that we might live through him."

In Romans 3:25, Christ's Atonement is critically mentioned: "Whom God hath set forth to be a propitiation through faith in his blood, to declare his righteousness for the remission of sins that are past, through the forbearance of God."

In John 11:25–26, Christ himself explained that he had to suffer and then rise from the dead the third day. He said, "I am the resurrection, and the life: he that believeth in me, though he were dead, yet shall he live: and whosoever liveth and believeth in me shall never die."

In 1 Corinthians 15:20–22, Christ's resurrection is explained: "Now is Christ risen from the dead, and become the firstfruits of them that slept. For since by man came death, by man came also the resurrection of the dead. For as in Adam all die, even so in Christ shall all be made alive." (See also Acts 26:23.)

Thus Christ's Atonement is universally beneficial. All will be made alive and benefit from the resurrection. In other words, we will all be resurrected with perfect bodies of flesh and bones, just like those of God and Christ. And, if we have exercised faith in Christ to the end, we will live forevermore with him and his Father. Thus we will have progressed from a spirit state to a mortal state and finally to an immortal, resurrected state.

In John 5:28–29 we read, "Marvel not at this: for the hour is coming, in the which all that are in the graves shall hear his voice, and shall come forth; they that have done good, unto the resurrection of life; and they that have done evil, unto the resurrection of damnation." (See also Acts 24:15.)

Remember Romans 5:12–18, which explains that the "free gift," the "gift of grace [the resurrection]" shall come "upon all men unto justification of life." This is so even though "all have sinned, and come short of the glory of God" (Romans 3:23).

WE MUST OVERCOME OUR SINS

All people sin and fall short of the glory of God, and "the wages of sin is death" (Romans 6:23). All people are subject to physical death and, insofar as we are removed from the presence of God, we suffer a temporary spiritual death. Christ, through his death and resurrection, unconditionally overcame the effects of Adam's sin. Christ is the firstfruits of them that slept. He ushered in the resurrection for all. In other words, Christ was the first to be resurrected and, because of him and his great atoning sacrifice, we too shall have the fruits of the resurrection (1 Corinthians 15:20–22).

We can overcome our sins, but only on condition that we repent, exercising our faith in Christ. If we do so, Christ's atoning sacrifice for us will absolve our sins and allow us once again to enter God's presence.

The doctrine of the Atonement represents the core of the gospel. The reasons Jesus could make the atoning sacrifice for us are

1. He was the Only Begotten of God in the flesh.
2. He was literally born of God.

MODERN REVELATION ON CHRIST'S SACRIFICE

The Book of Mormon is a great source of knowledge of Christ's atoning sacrifice for us.

In 2 Nephi 9:21–22, the Prophet Jacob stated of Christ: "He cometh into the world that he may save all men if they will hearken unto his voice; for behold, *he suffereth the pains of all men, yea, the pains of every living creature, both men, women, and children,* who belong to the family of Adam. And he suffereth this that the resurrection might pass upon all men, that all might stand before him at the great and judgment day."

We know that God has called prophets in these latter days. Some of their revelations are helpful in understanding the atoning sacrifice of Jesus Christ.

The Lord told the Prophet Joseph Smith, "I command you to repent—repent, lest I smite you by the rod of my mouth, and by my wrath, and by my anger, and your sufferings be sore—how sore you know not, how exquisite you know not, yea, how hard to bear you know not. For behold, *I, God, have suffered these things for all, that they might not suffer if they would repent; but if they would not repent they must suffer even as I; which suffering caused myself, even God, the greatest of all, to tremble because of pain, and to bleed at every pore, and to suffer both body and spirit—and would that I might not drink the bitter cup, and shrink*" (D&C 19:15–18).

Again the Lord said, "Remember the worth of souls is great in the sight of God; for, behold, the Lord your Redeemer suffered death in the flesh; wherefore *he suffered the pain of all men*, that all men might repent and come unto him. And he hath risen again from the dead, that he might bring all men unto him, on conditions of repentance. And how great is his joy in the soul that repenteth! Wherefore, you are called to cry repentance unto this people. And if it so be that you should labor all your days in crying repentance unto this people, and bring, save it be one soul unto me, how great shall be your joy with him in the kingdom of my Father! And now, if your joy will be great with one soul that you have brought unto me into the kingdom of my Father, how great will be your joy if you should bring many souls unto me!" (D&C 18:10–16)

The Book of Mormon prophet Jacob expanded the doctrine of the Atonement further: "It behooveth the great Creator that he suffereth himself to become subject unto man in the flesh, and die for all men, that all men might become subject unto him. For as death hath passed upon all men, to fulfil the merciful plan of the great Creator, there must needs be a power of resurrection, and the resurrection must needs come unto man by reason of the fall; and the fall came by reason of transgression; and because man became fallen they were cut off from the presence of the Lord. Wherefore, *it must needs be an infinite atonement—save it should be an infinite atonement this corruption could not put on incorruption. Wherefore, the first judgment which came upon man must needs have remained to an endless duration. And if so, this flesh must have laid down to rot and to crumble to its mother earth, to rise no more.* O the wisdom of God, his mercy and grace! For behold, if the flesh should rise no more our spirits must become subject to that angel who fell from before the presence of the Eternal God, and became the devil, to rise no more. And our spirits must have become like unto him, and we become devils, angels to a devil, to be shut out from the presence of our God, and to remain with the father of lies, in misery, like unto himself; yea, to that being who beguiled our first parents, who transformeth himself nigh unto an angel of light, and stirreth up the children of men unto secret combinations of murder and all manner of secret works of darkness. O how great the goodness of our God, who prepareth a way for our escape from the grasp of this awful monster; yea, that monster, death and hell, which I call the death of the body, and also the death of the spirit" (2 Nephi 9:5–10).

Had it not been for Jesus Christ and his atoning sacrifice, we would still be cut off from the presence of God. We would not be looking forward to the resurrection. We would have remained in a state of nonprogression, being subject to the devil's wiles. We would be shut out from the presence of God—miserable, with no hope. Through the Atonement of Christ, we are enabled to continually progress on the pathway to salvation and thus escape death, hell, and the grasp of Satan.

Again, in 2 Nephi 9:23–27, Jacob proclaims of the Lord: "He commandeth all men that they must repent, and be baptized in his name, having perfect faith in the Holy One of Israel, or they cannot be saved in the kingdom of God. And if they will not repent and believe in his name, and be baptized in his name, and endure to the end, they must be damned; for the Lord God, the Holy One of Israel, has spoken it. Wherefore, he has given a law; and where there is no law given there is no punishment; and where there is no punishment there is no condemnation; and where there is no condemnation the mercies of the Holy One of Israel have claim upon them, because of the Atonement; for they are delivered by the power of him. *For the atonement satisfieth the demands of his justice upon all those who have not the law given to them, that they are delivered from that awful monster, death and hell, and the devil, and the lake of fire and brimstone, which is endless torment; and they are restored to that God who gave them breath, which is the Holy One of Israel.* But wo unto him that has the law given, yea, that has all the commandments of God, like unto us, and that transgresseth them, and that wasteth the days of his probation, for awful is his state!"

In 2 Nephi 2:25–29, the Prophet Lehi instructs us: "Adam fell that men might be; and men are, that they might have joy. And the Messiah cometh in the fulness of time, that he may redeem the children of men from the fall. And because that they are redeemed from the fall they have become free forever, knowing good from evil; to act for themselves and not to be acted upon, save it be by the punishment of the law at the great and last day, according to the commandments which God hath given. Wherefore, men are free according to the flesh; and all things are given them which are expedient unto man. And they are free to choose liberty and eternal life, through the great Mediator of all men, or to choose captivity and death, according to the captivity and power of the devil; for he seeketh that all men might be miserable like unto himself. And now, my sons, I would that ye should look to the great Mediator, and hearken unto his great commandments; and be faithful unto his words, and choose eternal life, according to the will of his Holy Spirit; and not choose eternal death, according to the will of the flesh and the evil which is therein, which giveth the spirit of the devil power to captivate, to bring you down to hell, that he may reign over you in his own kingdom."

The prophet Amulek, in Alma 34:13–15, explains the Atonement in beautiful terms: "It is expedient that *there should be a great and last sacrifice,* and then shall there be, or it is expedient there should be, a stop to the shedding of blood; then shall the law of Moses be fulfilled; yea, it shall be all fulfilled, every jot and tittle, and none shall have passed away. And behold, this is the whole meaning of the law, every whit *pointing to that great and last sacrifice; and that great and last sacrifice will be the Son of God, yea, infinite and eternal. And thus he shall bring salvation to all those who shall believe on his name; this being the intent of this last sacrifice, to bring about the bowels of mercy, which overpowereth justice, and bringeth about means unto men that they may have faith unto repentance.*"

Through latter-day revelation, we are able to know more about Christ. We thus are able to more fully understand his atoning sacrifice. The Book of Mormon is particularly specific about what a Christian is. Virtually every page of that book testifies of Christ.

The atoning sacrifice of Jesus Christ brought full power to repent of our sins. It is frightening to imagine a future without an ability to have "faith unto repentance." If we could not repent of our sins, we would be living lives of degradation, being dragged down each day by our sins. But the Atonement of Jesus Christ brings us hope and salvation.

CHAPTER 6

THE NATURE
OF MORTALITY

There is consolation in the assurance that whatever becomes of this husk of a planet, the inner meaning of it, hope itself, God, man's ideal, continually progresses and develops.

—William Faulkner

Free will, though it makes evil possible, is also the only thing that makes possible any love or goodness or joy worth having.

—C. S. Lewis

MANY PEOPLE see no reason for our life on earth. They decry the hardship, travail, sickness, murder, crime, mental illness, war, rumors of war, and various indignities suffered by humanity. They ask, "What is the purpose of life? Why must we go through this experience with all of its ups and downs? Is there real meaning to this existence? Who are we?"

Many years ago, my missionary companion and I were teaching the gospel to a woman who had become, in essence, a recluse. She lived with her brother in a small house in the center of town, and she never left their home.

This woman raised parakeets. Entering her home was an interesting experience, because hundreds of birds were flying free inside.

Somehow, as frightened as this woman was by the outside world, she did allow us to enter her home. There, for many months, we taught her the gospel of Jesus Christ. She was extremely nervous each time we visited her, but she forced herself to listen and talk with us.

Gradually she came to love the gospel, and she diligently studied everything we gave her to read. In time, she could express her belief that the gospel teachings were true. Yet she would never attend church or ask for baptism.

Finally, I asked her why she was not willing to go to church and be baptized. Her response was devastating for her and for us.

She responded, "Elder Hatch, I'm not worthy of Christ's church. You once told me there are two unforgivable sins."

I responded, "Yes, blasphemy against the Holy Ghost, as described in Matthew 12:31, and murder wherein innocent blood is shed. I know that your testimony of Christ is not yet strong enough that you could commit blasphemy against the Holy Ghost. I'm also sure, as sensitive as you are, that you have not killed another human being."

She sighed and said, "Don't be so sure of the latter."

She told us of her marriage to a brutal husband who had abused her. She had become pregnant and, while bedridden, had suffered through a difficult pregnancy.

This woman loved birds. To hurt her, the vicious husband would bring birds home to the bedroom, break their wings, and leave them to flap around on the floor. Then he would let the cat in to kill them in front of his bedridden and sensitive wife. The trauma to this kind woman was emotionally debilitating. She had even felt that she was going out of her mind.

She had begun to hate her husband, and she certainly hadn't wanted to have his child. Then one day he suggested a way out of their undesirable marriage—he suggested she have an abortion. She had been so emotionally and physically ill that she had gone through with it. From that day on, she had lived with the dreaded feeling that she could never be forgiven for what she had done.

We carefully explained that, while God frowns on abortion on demand, he does grant us the gift of repentance so we can be forgiven of our sinful acts, including abortion. (See 3 Nephi 30:2.) She was so relieved. She cried tears of joy at God's kindness to her. She had repented for years and now felt that God could forgive her.

I seized the opportunity to tell her that we would pick her up for church the next Sunday. Before she could protest, we left her front porch. As we left, she shook like an autumn leaf about to fall.

My companion berated me all the way back to our apartment. He was afraid that on Sunday we would walk the two miles to her home in the snowy weather and she would not be ready to go. I told him to have faith.

When we arrived the next Sunday morning, she was a nervous wreck but was ready to go with us. At church she was so nervous that the uneven, four-legged chair she sat on in the humble church meeting place rattled throughout the meeting.

After the meeting, I promised her that if she would exert faith and regularly attend church, all of her nervousness and fears would leave her within a year. The next year was difficult for her, but she was faithful. By the end of the year, all of her fears were gone, and she became an active member of the faith and one of the great genealogists of the Church.

Shortly after I left my mission, my wife, Elaine, and I were visiting Brigham Young University when this woman came to Utah and attended the general conference of the Church with eight thousand other people in the Mormon Tabernacle. She was amazingly calm, and I was excited to see the fulfillment of my earlier promise. She was finally at peace with herself, her community, and the world. She had fully embraced the gospel of Jesus Christ and found the purpose of her life.

We lived as spirit children of God before this world was created. We shouted for joy at the opportunity of coming to earth. We knew it would be beneficial for us to have this earthly experience. We can progress here, if we will, through our beliefs and our actions. (See Job 38:4–7.)

LUCIFER AND HIS ANGELS

Lucifer, or Satan, also was a spirit son of God. But, with his followers—other children of God—he rebelled against our Heavenly Father and was cast out from his presence. Because of this, he will not have the opportunity to obtain a body of flesh and bones and become like God. Nor will he have the opportunity to live again in God's presence.

Isaiah 14:12–15 states, "How art thou fallen from heaven, O Lucifer, son of the morning! how art thou cut down to the ground, which didst weaken the nations! For thou hast said in thine heart, I will ascend into heaven, I will exalt my throne above the stars of God: I will sit also upon the mount of the congregation, in the sides of the north: I will ascend above the heights of the clouds; I will be like the most high. Yet thou shalt be brought down to hell, to the sides of the pit."

The Apostle Peter confirms this in 2 Peter 2:4: "God spared not the angels that sinned, but cast them down to hell, and delivered them into chains of darkness, to be reserved unto judgment."

This is also mentioned in Jude 1:6: "The angels which kept not their first estate, but left their own habitation, he hath reserved in everlasting chains under darkness unto the judgment of the great day." By the "first estate," the Bible means our premortal existence.

We who live on earth were supporters of God. We kept our first estate and were therefore qualified to come here, outside the presence of God, where we can make a freewill choice to accept or reject his gospel. Satan and his followers, however, rebelled against this plan. In fact, there was a war in heaven in which the righteous spirit sons and daughters of God fought against Satan and his angels.

In Revelation 12:7–9 we read, "There was war in heaven: Michael and his angels fought against the dragon; and the dragon fought and his angels, and prevailed not; neither was their place found any more in heaven. And the great dragon was cast out, that old serpent, called the Devil, and Satan, which deceiveth the whole world: he was cast out into the earth, and his angels were cast out with him."

Satan and his angels will never have the opportunity to gain physical bodies and become more like God. They will always remain spirits. They would like bodies but will never enjoy the privilege of having them.

In Matthew 8:28–32, we read that Christ came into the country of the Gergesenes and met two men possessed with devils. The men came out of the tombs, "exceeding fierce, so that no man might pass by that way." The evil spirits immediately recognized Jesus as the Son of God and "cried out, saying, What have we to do with thee, Jesus, thou Son of God? art thou come hither to torment us before the time?" These spirits wanted bodies so much that they "besought him, saying, If thou cast us out, suffer us to go away into the herd of swine. And he said unto them, Go. And when they were come out, they went into the herd of swine: and, behold, the whole herd of swine ran violently down a steep place into the sea, and perished in the waters."

People who think all they must do to be saved is to believe in Jesus Christ need to consider this story. The evil spirits believed in Jesus. In fact, they knew he was the Christ. But they were permanently cast out of the presence of God. Thus we see that belief—mere intellectual assent—is not enough for salvation, for even "the devils . . . believe, and tremble" (James 2:19).

Those who *really* believe will live Christ's gospel and endure to the end in his service (Matthew 10:22).

REASONS FOR OUR LIFE ON EARTH

In the premortal war in heaven, we followed God and his eldest Son, Jesus Christ, and we "shouted for joy" (Job 38:7) at the opportunity of coming to earth.

There were two reasons we did these things.

1. We wanted to obtain a body of flesh and bones so we could become more like our Father in Heaven.

2. We needed to be tested outside the presence of God to see if we would live the commandments and make the right choices. We wanted the opportunity to choose for ourselves the kind of people we would become. Now here we are. By exercising our moral agency here on earth, we determine our future in eternity.

Keep in mind that a veil has been drawn over our minds. We cannot look back and see the great plans in which we participated before the world was created. If we could, this life would not be a freewill test to see whether we will live worthy to be with God forever.

MORTAL BODIES

God sent us to earth and gave us bodies of flesh and bones for a divine purpose. This earthly existence gives us the opportunity to work out our salvation with fear and trembling. In gaining bodies of flesh and bones, we are in an eternal process of becoming more like our Father in Heaven.

Ultimately, our bodies will be resurrected like Christ's (1 Corinthians 15:20–22). Our bodies are important in God's and in our eyes. Shouldn't we, therefore, keep them clean and unspotted from the world?

Since Christ was resurrected with his body of flesh and bones (Luke 24:36–39), we also will be resurrected with our bodies of flesh and bones. Perhaps that is why Paul, in 1 Corinthians 3:16–17, said, "Know ye not that ye are the temple of God, and that the Spirit of God dwelleth in you? If any man defile the temple of God, him shall God destroy; for the temple of God is holy, which temple ye are."

One reason we should not take unclean things into our bodies is because God has compared them to his temple. He wants us to keep them clean from the sins of this world. We must live the rules of health so that we can keep our bodies clean and so we will not be tempted to do the things of the world. How we treat our physical bodies is important. We must keep our temples of God holy and pure by living moral and spiritual laws, as well as the physical laws of health. Through a latter-day revelation called the Word of Wisdom, we are prohibited from drinking alcohol, abusing drugs, using tobacco, drinking tea or coffee, or partaking of anything debilitating to our bodies, minds, and souls. Modern doctors also advocate such wise health concepts.

Even so, we are given our agency to do what we want. But we will naturally pay the price for doing what is not God's will.

MORAL AGENCY

In this day of moral relativism and political correctness, many have difficulty discerning between right and wrong. True religion helps us understand the difference and aids us in our moral choices.

We have had our agency from the beginning. Even Adam and Eve were given the right to choose: "The Lord God commanded the man, saying, Of every tree of the garden thou mayest freely eat: but of the tree of the knowledge of good and evil, thou shalt not eat of it: for in the day that thou eatest thereof thou shalt surely die" (Genesis 2:16–17). And in Deuteronomy 11:26–28 we read, "I set before you this day a blessing and a curse; a blessing, if ye obey the commandments of the Lord your God, which I command you this day: and a curse, if ye will not obey the commandments of the Lord your God, but turn aside out of the way which I command you this day, to go after other gods, which ye have not known." (See also Deuteronomy 30:15–19.) We also read, "Choose you this day whom ye will serve; . . .but as for me and my house, we will serve the Lord" (Joshua 24:15; see also 1 Kings 18:21; Jonah 1–4; Galatians 6:7–8).

God's plan of salvation provides us the freedom to choose what we will be and how we will live. We are given this freedom as a test in making our own choices outside the presence of God. Now we are here, to "work out our own salvation with fear and trembling" (Philippians 2:12). If we do so, following God in word and deed, the day will come when we will return to his presence.

CHAPTER 7

COMMANDMENTS WE ARE TO LIVE

He who thinks to reach God by running away from the world,
when and where does he expect to meet Him?

—TAGORE

TO HELP US RETURN to his presence and teach us how we are to live, God has given us the holy scriptures. The scriptures are a guide to gospel laws that God expects us to live. If we live them, we will have the privilege of living with God forever. It is up to us. We make the choice by the way we live after we receive the gospel of Jesus Christ.

THE LAW OF MOSES

Although Christ came to fulfill the law of Moses, he did not ignore the importance of the Old Testament laws, for he said, "Think not that I am come to destroy the law, or the prophets: I am not come to destroy, but to fulfil. For verily I say unto you, Till heaven and earth pass, one jot or one tittle shall in no wise pass from the law, till all be fulfilled" (Matthew 5:17–18).

Paul explained in Galatians 3:24–27, "The law was our schoolmaster to bring us unto Christ, that we might be justified by faith. But after that faith is come, we are no longer under a schoolmaster. For ye are all the children of God by faith in Christ Jesus. For as many of you as have been baptized into Christ have put on Christ." These statements show that the law of Moses was a preparatory law to bring us to Christ—to prepare us for Christ.

In response to the Pharisee's question, "Master, which is the great commandment in the law?" Christ said, "Thou shalt love the Lord thy God with all thy heart, and with all thy soul, and with all thy mind. This is the first and great commandment. And the second is like unto it, Thou shalt love thy neighbour as thyself" (Matthew 22:36–39).

In John 13:34, Christ said, "A new commandment I give unto you, That ye love one another; as I have loved you, that ye also love one another."

In John 14:15, he said, "If ye love me, keep my commandments."

What were the commandments to which Christ was referring?

THE TEN COMMANDMENTS

We begin with the Ten Commandments listed in Exodus 20:3–17. Remember, the Lord wrote, with his own finger, the Ten Commandments on tablets of stone (Exodus 31:18). These Ten Commandments represent the basic laws of God, from which come almost all other civil and religious laws. The Ten Commandments form the basis for all ethical human conduct.

Commandment 1: "Thou shalt have no other gods before me" (Exodus 20:3).

Some people worship politics, wealth, sports, sex, and many other things as their gods. But we cannot afford to place any worldly endeavor or objects above or in place of the true God. We are to worship only the true God who was earlier described in this book. According to Christ, he must be our first priority, above all else: "He that loveth father or mother more than me is not worthy of me: and he that loveth son or daughter more than me is not worthy of me" (Matthew 10:37). Christ further explained, "Seek ye first the kingdom of God, and his righteousness" (Matthew 6:33). I believe that Clarke's *Bible Commentary*, 1:402–3, states this principle well: "This commandment prohibits every species of mental idolatry, and all inordinate attachment to earthly and sensible things . . . God is the foundation of happiness, and no intelligent creature can be happy but through him . . . The very first commandment of the whole series is divinely calculated to prevent man's misery and promote his happiness, by taking him off from all false dependence, and leading him to God himself, the fountain of all good."

Commandment 2: "Thou shalt not make unto thee any graven image, or any likeness of any thing that is in heaven above, or that is in the earth beneath, or that is in the water under the earth: Thou shalt not bow down thyself to them, nor serve them" (Exodus 20:4–5).

Many "gods" have been worshiped by mankind—from gods of metal to gods of wood, fabric, chrome, and stone. Modern idols range from businesses to automobiles, clothes, homes, pleasure boats, and numerous other material things. Also, immaterial things like titles, degrees, and worldly honors may constitute idols. We all know people who worship sports, activities, power, prestige, and money.

Regardless of what we desire and admire, we must place God first—above all material or immaterial things, goals, pursuits, activities, or feelings. We must continually work at this; yet, the longer we live, the more we realize that the most important matters center on what God has asked us to do, not on the transitory winnings of the world.

Commandment 3: "Thou shalt not take the name of the Lord thy God in vain; for the Lord will not hold him guiltless that taketh his name in vain" (Exodus 20:7).

This commandment has two main aspects: (1) an implication that God's children are expected to have reverence for him and his name, and (2) an integral part of the gospel consisting of oaths and covenants with God.

How many of us have heard others use God's name in vain for emphasis or dramatic effect, or out of frustration, anger, or habit? All false oaths are prohibited by this commandment. Common swearing and using God's name in vain, including all light and irreverent uses of God's name, are forbidden. How can we approach God in prayer after having desecrated his name? Reverence and profanity are inconsistent and incompatible. When we accept baptism, we enter into a covenant with God to take Christ's name upon ourselves. We agree to abide by God's laws in part because he remits our sins.

This commandment also means we should not speak lightly of God or use his name in frivolous ways. He will not hold us guiltless if we do these things.

Commandment 4: "Remember the sabbath day, to keep it holy" (Exodus 20:8).

Here we are commanded to work six days and rest the seventh. This commandment promotes both work and worship. The seventh day is to be set aside to worship God. The Hebrew word *Shabbat*, from which we get the word *Sabbath*, means "rest" or "the cessation of labor." The Sabbath began with the creation of the world, wherein the Lord worked for six days and then rested from his labor.

The Sabbath is so important that in Old Testament times, breaking the Sabbath was punishable by death. (See Rushdoony, *Institutes of Biblical Law*, page 137.) The Sabbath was so important in pre-Christian times that the Lord called it "a sign between me and you" (Exodus 31:13).

In ancient Israel, observing the Sabbath applied to servants (employees), family members, and animals. Even the land was subject to the Sabbath and was given rest every seventh year (Exodus 20:10; Leviticus 25:2–7).

Commandment 5: "Honour thy father and thy mother: that thy days may be long upon the land which the Lord thy God giveth thee" (Exodus 20:12).

The family rises to the forefront in this commandment. When parents are God-fearing people and live in righteousness, generally children honor and revere them. What about unrighteous parents? One might honor them by living exemplary lives. In Ephesians 6:1 we read, "Children, obey your parents in the Lord: for this is right." The next verse says, "Honour thy father and mother."

To obey one's parents means to obey them in righteousness. We, by our own lives, can honor our parents, whether or not they deserve that honor.

Commandment 6: "Thou shalt not kill" (Exodus 20:13).

The sin of murder, or the willful destruction of human life, is one of the most serious crimes against God's law. By taking another's life, the murderer takes away another person's opportunity to "work out . . . salvation with fear and trembling" (Philippians 2:12).

What about killing in war? The Lord understands our obligations to uphold the sovereignty of our nation and to fight against evil and the aggressions of others. We must "render therefore unto Caesar the things which are Caesar's; and unto God the things that are God's" (Matthew 22:21). The very implications of that statement are rife with philosophical contradictions. We must give obedience to sovereign laws, but we also have the obligation to keep the laws of God, which take precedence. That is most difficult. There were many Christians fighting on all sides during World War II, as well as in most other wars. Naturally, we have to wonder about Christians who carried out the genocidal orders of Hitler and others, which were contrary to this commandment.

Commandment 7: "Thou shalt not commit adultery"
(Exodus 20:14).

Women and men have the power of choice and, with this right, can exercise their impulses for righteous or evil actions. We have always possessed the right of choice. Yet, we need to understand that there are right choices and wrong choices. As the spirit children of God, we have an obligation to make the right choices.

Satan and his minions exercised their right of choice in the premortal existence and rebelled against God's wishes. We exercised ours to come to earth and complete this part of our progression, outside the presence of God but with his influence through the scriptures, the prophets, and inspiration.

God expects us to sanctify the marriage covenant and to honor each other by not committing adultery. The covenant of marriage is a sacred institution given women and men so they can reproduce and give other spirits the opportunity to come to the earth. Christ was very explicit on this subject (Matthew 5:28).

Christ extended this law to fornication as well (Matthew 15:19). In 1 Corinthians 6:9, the Lord said, "Know ye not that the unrighteous shall not inherit the kingdom of God? Be not deceived: neither fornicators, nor idolaters, nor adulterers, nor effeminate, nor abusers of themselves with mankind."

Adultery is one of the most serious sins because the institution of marriage and family is sacred in the eyes of God. Adultery is considered second only to murder. Sexual intimacy is to be reserved for marriage partners. To breach the solemn obligation to remain true to one's marriage partner is a heinous sin. Adultery splits couples apart, causes children to be raised by only one parent, debilitates the family, spreads disease, and results in the breakdown of civilized society.

Moral fidelity, before and after marriage, exalts the marriage compact, elevates the relationship between man and woman, strengthens the family relationship, and strengthens the community. We believe it is essential to a spiritual relationship with God.

Again, as Paul wrote in Galatians 5:19–21, "The works of the flesh are manifest, which are these; adultery, fornication, uncleanness, lasciviousness, idolatry, witchcraft, hatred, variance, emulations, wrath, strife, seditions, heresies, envyings, murders, drunkenness, revellings, and such like: of the which I tell you before, as I have also told you in time past, that they which do such things shall not inherit the kingdom of God."

Adultery consists of stealing another's virtue. In the case of adultery, we cannot give back that person's lost virtue. It is easy to see why adultery and murder are such heinous sins in the eyes of God. No matter how hard we try, we cannot give back another person's life or virtue.

I know of a number of instances where fathers have committed incest with their daughters. It is difficult to understand how this could happen, but it has. In each case, the daughter suffered severe anxiety and emotional difficulties. In a real sense, the daughter's sense of well-being has been stolen by this offensive conduct. It is extremely difficult for these young women ever to feel right again. Their virtue has been stolen under the worst of circumstances—no fault of their own. Their fathers will pay the spiritual price.

Commandment 8: "Thou shalt not steal" (Exodus 20:15).

This commandment consists of only four words but is profound because it covers many aspects of moral life. Stealing can exist in a great variety of circumstances, not just in taking another's property. The Lord condemns all thievery and dishonesty in the simple command "Thou shalt not steal." Whether it is in the form of shoplifting, misusing food stamps, or stealing another's virtue or reputation, it is wrong.

Commandment 9: "Thou shalt not bear false witness against thy neighbor" (Exodus 20:16).

This commandment is broken time and time again. It seems not as significant as the commandments forbidding murder, adultery, and stealing, but it is just as important. All it takes to bear false witness is to disseminate false rumors, speculations, insinuations, distortions, or misrepresentations. Murder takes a human life and thus prevents someone from fulfilling his or her destiny on earth. But bearing false witness chips away at a person's character. To ruin another's reputation is also a serious offense.

Commandment 10: "Thou shalt not covet thy neighbor's house, thou shalt not covet thy neighbour's wife, nor his manservant, nor his maidservant, nor his ox, nor his ass, nor any thing that is thy neighbor's" (Exodus 20:17).

All the other commandments can be broken through the sin of coveting. If we covet material things, we can make them our gods and, in essence, bow down before them. A coveter can be crude, curse, take God's name in vain, desecrate the Sabbath, fail to support his mother and father in need, kill to get gain, lust after a neighbor's wife or husband, steal, and bear false witness to obtain gain. Almost all these commandments are tied together, and breaking one may amount to the breaking of others.

Certainly, we can have the desire to improve our circumstances through honest ambition. We can admire our neighbor's possessions.

But we have the obligation to work for good things through honest and lawful means.

Paul once equated coveting with idolatry. In Ephesians 5:5 he said, "No whoremonger, nor unclean person, nor covetous man, who is an idolater, hath any inheritance in the kingdom of Christ and of God." (See also Colossians 3:5.) If we covet worldly things so much that our allegiance to God and his principles diminishes or vanishes, then we are worshiping material things above God. Then we are idolaters.

In 1 Samuel 15:23, the Prophet Samuel advised King Saul that sin and iniquity amounted to idolatry.

All aspects of moral behavior are covered by the Ten Commandments, which are enduring rules of conduct for us all. All prophets have taught these commandments. I believe they existed even before the world began.

Jesus said, "Thou shalt love the Lord thy God with all thy heart, and with all thy soul, and with all thy mind. This is the first and great commandment. And the second is like unto it, Thou shalt love thy neighbour as thyself" (Matthew 22:37–39). These two great commandments embrace every one of the Ten Commandments.

The Ten Commandments lay the foundation for Christian belief. Mormons subscribe fully to them.

The Ten Commandments are basically negative commandments. Eight out of the ten tell what we should not do rather than what we should do. The Ten Commandments are broad, general principles. In the preface to the Ten Commandments (Exodus 20:2), the Lord said, "I am the Lord thy God, which have brought thee out of the land of Egypt, *out of the house of bondage*." In spite of their negative tone, living the Ten Commandments can keep us free from spiritual and physical bondage.

Paul said the law was "our schoolmaster to bring us unto Christ" (Galatians 3:24). He was referring to the Mosaic law, a broad list of rules and laws to which the children of Israel became subject. When Christ came to earth, he fulfilled the law, and his Christian teachings became the higher law to the Mosaic lower laws of performances and obligations as described in Exodus and Leviticus. Therefore, we are no longer subject to all of the rigid rules, ordinances, and performances required of ancient Israel. But we must study Christ's admonitions to us and, in the process, live Christian lives.

If we live the Ten Commandments, we are doing much to progress back into the presence of God. But as important as the Ten Commandments are, keeping them is only part of what we must do to inherit the kingdom of God.

CHAPTER 8

FAITH

Faith is the antiseptic of the soul.

—WALT WHITMAN

SINCE WE ARE HERE on the earth to progress, gain a body, and become more like our Father in Heaven, what steps must we take to go back into his presence? First, we must have faith in God. Faith is the first principle of the gospel; it must be obtained through trust and confidence in a higher being and his plan of salvation as articulated in his scriptures.

We must have faith in God in order to make the right decisions in life. Paul said, "Faith is the substance [that is, confidence] of things hoped for, the evidence of things not seen" (Hebrews 11:1). He also said, "Without faith it is impossible to please [God]: for he that cometh to God must believe that he is, and that he is a rewarder of them that diligently seek him" (Hebrews 11:6). Paul further stated, "By faith Noah . . . prepared an ark to the saving of his house"; "By faith Abraham, when he was tried, offered up Isaac"; "By faith Isaac blessed Jacob and Esau"; "By faith Jacob . . . worshiped, leaning upon the top of his staff"; "By faith Joseph, when he died, made mention of the departing of the children of Israel"; "By faith [Moses] forsook Egypt"; "By faith they passed through the Red sea as by dry land"; and "By faith the walls of Jericho fell down, after they were compassed about seven days" (Hebrews 11:7–30).

Paul said in Romans 10:17, "Faith cometh by hearing, and hearing by the word of God."

In Romans 1:16–17 Paul wrote, "I am not ashamed of the gospel of Christ: for it is the power of God unto salvation to every one that believeth; to the Jew first, and also to the Greek. For therein is the righteousness of God revealed from faith to faith: as it is written, The just shall live by faith."

In 2 Corinthians 5:7 he said, "We walk by faith, not by sight."

Jesus stated in Matthew 21:21, "If ye have faith, and doubt not, . . . if ye shall say unto this mountain, Be thou removed, and be thou cast into the sea; it shall be done."

IS BELIEF ENOUGH TO SATISFY THE REQUISITES OF SALVATION?

Many Christians define faith as simply accepting Jesus as our personal Savior. If we do this, they say, full and complete salvation is assured. They are convinced that mere belief qualifies us to be saved in the kingdom of God. That is a misinterpretation of the scriptures.

For instance, Paul says in Acts 16:30–31 that if we believe on Jesus Christ, we will be saved. Yet later in the same chapter, he makes it clear that baptism is a prerequisite for salvation when the jailer and his whole family are baptized.

John 3:16 says, "God so loved the world, that he gave his only begotten Son, that whosoever believeth in him should not perish, but have everlasting life." Many interpret this to mean that mere belief is enough to assure salvation in the kingdom of God.

Yet this scriptural interpretation is clarified earlier in John 3:3–5: "Jesus answered and said unto [Nicodemus], Verily, verily, I say unto thee, Except a man be born again, he cannot see the kingdom of God. Nicodemus saith unto him, How can a man be born when he is old? can he enter the second time into his mother's womb, and be born? Jesus answered, Verily, verily, I say unto thee, Except a man be born of water and of the Spirit, he cannot enter into the kingdom of God." These verses make it clear that we must do more than merely believe. We must be baptized both of water and of the Spirit.

WILL ONLY A SELECT FEW BE SAVED BY GRACE ONLY?

Ephesians 2:8–10 is often cited to show that we are "saved by grace alone" and not by our works. Some have even taught that only a select few are predetermined to be "saved by grace." However, we must look at all of Paul's writings to fully understand what these scriptures in Ephesians mean.

In Ephesians 2:8–10 Paul states: "By grace are ye saved through faith; and that not of yourselves: it is the gift of God: not of works, lest any man should boast. For we are his workmanship, created in Christ Jesus unto good works, which God hath before ordained that we should walk in them."

The founder of the Lutheran Church, Martin Luther, interpreted Ephesians 2:8–10 to mean that man is "justified by faith" only.

Calvin, one of the founders of the Presbyterian Church, interpreted these scriptures to mean that only a select few will be saved in the kingdom of God—those to whom God arbitrarily gives his grace.

Really, are only a few of us to be arbitrarily saved by grace?

Paul, the author of the epistle to the Ephesians, clarifies this concept earlier in the Bible in Romans 5:12–18. There he states: "As by one man sin entered into the world, and death by sin; and so death passed upon all men, for that all have sinned: . . . But not as the offence, so also *is the free gift.* For if through the offence of one many be dead, much more the *grace of God, and the gift by grace,* which is by one man, Jesus Christ, hath *abounded unto many.* . . . Therefore as by the offence of one judgment came upon all men to condemnation; even so by the righteousness of one the free gift came upon *all men* unto justification of life."

Note that the language of "grace," "gift of God," "the free gift," "grace of God," and "gift by grace" are the same in Paul's writings in both Ephesians and Romans. Yet Romans makes it clear that this free gift, this gift by grace, not only "aboundeth to many" but is upon "all men." *This gift of grace of Jesus Christ will be received by everyone.* Not everyone will be saved, so this must not mean salvation in the kingdom of God.

1 Corinthians 15:20–22 establishes what this free gift to all people is. "Now is Christ risen from the dead, and become the firstfruits of them that slept. For since by man came death, by man came also the resurrection of the dead. For as in Adam all die, *even so in Christ shall all be made alive.*"

Clearly, when Paul talked about the grace of Christ or the free gift

Christ is going to give to all of us, he was talking about the resurrection. That is the only free gift given to all who come to the earth.

That gift comes because of the grace of Jesus Christ and the atoning sacrifice he made for us. Christ and our Father want us, as resurrected beings, to come back into their presence. However, although we will all have the free gift of resurrection, we must still "work out our own salvation with fear and trembling" (Philippians 2:12) in order to live with our Father (be ultimately saved) for eternity.

There are many other things we must do in mortality in addition to believing. Faith is more than mere belief. Faith is an *active* belief that motivates us to live the gospel of Jesus Christ.

James 2:14–20 states, "What doth it profit, my brethren, though a man say he hath faith, and have not works? can faith save him? If a brother or sister be naked, and destitute of daily food, and one of you say unto them, Depart in peace, be ye warmed and filled; notwithstanding ye give them not those things which are needful to the body; what doth it profit? Even so faith, if it hath not works, is dead, being alone. Yea, a man may say, Thou hast faith, and I have works: shew me thy faith without thy works, and I will shew thee my faith by my works. Thou believest that there is one God; thou doest well: the devils also believe, and tremble. But wilt thou know, O vain man, that faith without works is dead?"

Faith and belief are different. Belief is passive—a person may believe something but not be motivated to do something about that belief. Faith is dynamic. It compels us to do something about our belief.

A farmer may believe that if he plants corn, it will grow and be capable of harvest. But if he never actually plants it, he will reap nothing, no matter how sincere his belief. However, if he has faith in the harvest, he will not only believe, but he will also actually plant his corn and then harvest it.

Faith is an active belief. Faith impels us to action. Faith motivates us to live Christ's gospel—to do what is right. One of the great thinkers and scholars in the Mormon Church was James E. Talmage, a modern member of the Quorum of the Twelve Apostles, who defined faith as "vivified, vitalized, living belief" (*Articles of Faith* [Salt Lake City: Deseret Book, 1984], 88).

Some teach that if we merely believe, we will be saved in the kingdom of God. Furthermore, they say that once we are saved, we will go to heaven regardless of what else we may do here on the earth. That surely is not so. Mere belief is not enough.

In Galatians 5:19–21, Paul gives us a litany of things that will keep us out of the kingdom of heaven regardless of how "saved" we think we are: "The works of the flesh are manifest, which are these; adultery, fornication, uncleanness, lasciviousness, idolatry, witchcraft, hatred, variance, emulations, wrath, strife, seditions, heresies, envyings, murders, drunkenness, revellings, and such like: of the which I tell you before, as I have also told you in time past, *that they which do such things shall not inherit the kingdom of God.*"

Christ gave us explicit directions about how to know if his doctrine is true. "My doctrine is not mine, but his that sent me. If any man will do his will, he shall know of the doctrine, whether it be of God, or whether I speak of myself" (John 7:16–17). He also said, "Not every one that saith unto me, Lord, Lord, shall enter into the kingdom of heaven; but he that doeth the will of my Father which is in heaven" (Matthew 7:21).

In Mark 9:17–29 is the story of a father with a son who could not speak. The father brought his son to Christ. According to the father's description of the son's "dumb spirit," "he foameth, and gnasheth with his teeth," he "pineth away." Before the Savior, "he fell on the ground, and wallowed foaming." The father said that "ofttimes it hath cast him into the fire, and into the waters, to destroy him." The father finally exclaimed, "If thou canst do any thing, have compassion on us, and help us." Christ said, "If thou canst believe, all things are possible to him that believeth." The humble and believing father cried out, "Lord, I believe; help thou mine unbelief." The father was destitute of faith yet terrified of skepticism. Christ charged the dumb spirit to come out of the boy, and the spirit "rended" the boy "sore" to the extent that the people nearby thought the boy was dead. "But Jesus took him by the hand, and lifted him up; and he arose." Christ's disciples wondered why they, having been ordained by Christ, could not cast out this dumb spirit. Christ's simple answer was, "This kind can come forth by nothing, but by prayer and fasting." It took more than the disciples' belief. It took real faith engendered by "prayer and fasting."

Another example is in Matthew 9:20–22 (see also Mark 5:25–34 and Luke 8:43–48), where "a woman, which was diseased with an issue of blood twelve years, came behind [Jesus], and touched the hem of his garment: for she said within herself, If I may but touch his garment, I shall be whole. But Jesus turned him about, and when he saw her he said, Daughter, be of good comfort; thy faith hath made thee whole. And the woman was made whole from that hour."

In Mark's account (Mark 5:30), "Jesus, immediately knowing in himself that virtue had gone out of him, turned him about in the press, and said, Who touched my clothes?" The disciples were amazed he would ask such a question, since he was surrounded by a multitude and many were touching his clothes. However, the Lord recognized the woman's faith and responded to it.

He will do the same for us if we exercise faith in him by believing and living his teachings.

THE POWER OF FAITH

A good friend shared with me the story of David Hunter Perkins, a Cary Grant look-alike dry farmer who raised thoroughbred horses in the small southeastern Idaho town of Montpelier.

Dave, as his friends called him, took great pride in showing his city-reared grandchildren the simple joys of the Bear Lake County Fair. With their small hands grasping Grandpa's strong ones, they cherished the annual outing. One particular year they talked Grandpa into spending a nickel for a handful of colorful balloons tied securely to wooden sticks.

In the evening beside the overgrown rhubarb in his backyard, Dave masterfully crafted bows and arrows from the sticks. It was time that Mike, age six, and Jo, age four, learned the sport of archery. Dave's safety instructions were explicit, so he had no concern when Mike headed into the house to teach Jo how to shoot.

But as quickly as Mike shot the sharp arrow into the bedroom closet, Jo moved to retrieve it, and the arrow penetrated Jo's eye.

Not knowing what else to do, Jo's parents wrapped their tiny daughter in a blanket. Mom held her in the back seat of the car, and Dad headed for Salt Lake City, where an ophthalmologist met them at St. Mark's Hospital.

His diagnosis was devastating. The eye could not be saved. Plans were set for the doctor to remove it the following day.

Jo's parents, devout members of the Church, would not accept the prognosis. They immediately got in contact with a Mormon in the hospital, and within the hour two young elders and Jo's dad placed their hands upon Jo's head. In their blessing they promised in faith that the eye would be saved.

The following morning the doctor removed the patch and exclaimed that he had witnessed a miracle. No surgery would be required.

We all exercise faith daily. We get out of bed, eat our food, go to work, play with our friends and family, attend church, and live by various principles. We would not do these things if we had no faith in them.

The Apostle James defines faith as being made perfect by works. He cites a truism: "Thou believest that there is one God; thou doest well: the devils also believe, and tremble. But wilt thou know, O vain man, that faith without works is dead?" (James 2:19–20)

As you will recall, in Matthew 8:28–32 Christ came into the country of the Gergesenes, where he met "two possessed with devils, coming out of the tombs, exceeding fierce, so that no man might pass by that way." The evil spirits cried out, "What have we to do with thee, Jesus, thou Son of God? art thou come hither to torment us before the time?" They knew Jesus was the Christ. They recognized him. They believed in him. They wanted bodies so badly that they beseeched him to cast them into the bodies of a herd of swine. Christ simply said, "Go," and "they went into the herd of swine: and, behold, the whole herd of swine ran violently down a steep place into the sea, and perished in the waters."

We can learn much from this story. Remember, a third of the hosts of heaven refused to follow God and Christ and were "cast out" with Lucifer, the Son of the Morning. They will never have the privilege of obtaining bodies of flesh and bones so as to become like our Father in Heaven and the resurrected Christ. Here, they wanted bodies so badly that they would even have accepted the bodies of pigs. Even so, when they were cast into the swine, their nature took over, and they destroyed the swine, something they would do to us if we made ourselves vulnerable to them. These confessions of the evil spirits that Jesus was the Christ, the Messiah, showed they had actual knowledge and belief. Yet, their knowledge did not bring about a transformation of their evil natures. Thus, knowledge alone may be of no use at all. As James E. Talmage said, "Knowledge is to wisdom what belief is to faith, one an abstract principle, the other a living application. Not possession, but the proper use of knowledge constitutes wisdom" (*Articles of Faith*, 90).

Christ fervently recognized faith: "They brought to him a man sick of the palsy, lying on a bed: and Jesus seeing their faith said unto the sick of the palsy; Son, be of good cheer; thy sins be forgiven thee" (Matthew 9:2). What a revelation—"*thy sins be forgiven thee.*" This is one of the few instances showing that faith is so powerful that even sins can be forgiven through it.

Paul emphasized faith as one of three essential aspects of gospel belief: faith, hope, and charity (1 Corinthians 13). He placed all three in the highest category of gospel observance, even though he said that charity—love—is the greatest of the three.

If we willfully sin, wantonly do wrong, we will not have the sincerity to have faith or pray effectively. Our prayers will not be sincere. Our "faith" will be without the appropriate works, and therefore shallow.

Paul said there is "one Lord, one faith, one baptism" (Ephesians 4:5). Today, we have many interpretations of what the "Lord" is and what "faith" is, and we have at least eight different forms of "Christian" baptisms. In fact, there are more than eight hundred different Christian churches, all teaching their own doctrines, differing from one another, and, in many cases, contradicting each other. Most claim to be the one true church of Christ. We feel blessed because, through revelation from Christ, we have been given the opportunity to learn the true gospel of Jesus Christ and are led and counseled by those holding the priesthood of God.

The Apostle James stated: "If any of you lack wisdom, let him ask of God, that giveth to all men liberally, and upbraideth not; and it shall be given him. But let him ask in faith, nothing wavering. For he that wavereth is like a wave of the sea driven with the wind and tossed" (James 1:5–6).

We can pray for faith by asking "in faith." Faith is the gift of God to us, and God will not hesitate to strengthen our faith if we do the things he has commanded.

CHAPTER 9

REPENTANCE

He who has committed a sin and has repented, is freed from that sin, but he is purified only by the resolution of ceasing to sin and thinking "I will do so no more."

—CODE OF MANU (BETWEEN 1200 AND 500 BC)

SOMETIMES WE DON'T DO the things God has commanded. All of us sin from time to time. That is why one of the greatest principles of Christianity is the principle of repentance. Without the opportunity for forgiveness, we would all be in a constant state of depression. There would be no hope. Certainly I work at repentance all the time. We all should. I have many failings and, realizing that God will forgive and accept me, it is worth the effort to overcome these personal failings.

When I served as a bishop in my church, a man came to me in total depression over sins he had committed. He had been unfaithful to his wife and family. He felt there was no hope for him and was about to commit suicide. He was thrilled when I explained to him that the Lord understands our difficulties and has provided a means for us to repent. I told him, "You must have the faith to begin that sometimes long process of repentance. If you will, the Lord will forgive you, and you can start anew to reach the spiritual heights you desire."

In Acts 2:37–38, Peter, assuming we have faith, states the first principles and ordinances of the gospel: "They were pricked in their heart, and said unto Peter and to the rest of the apostles, Men and brethren, what shall we do? Then Peter said unto them, Repent, and be baptized every one of you in the name of Jesus Christ for the remission of sins, and ye shall receive the gift of the Holy Ghost."

In order to progress in the plan of salvation, we must live the first principles and ordinances of the gospel. Once we have faith in Christ, we must repent of our sins. And this we must do before we can participate in the ordinances of the gospel.

A repentant person, exercising faith, makes a change in her or his life. The change must be for the better and involves repentance—a sorrowful recognition of sin or error that brings about a reformation in that person's life.

THE PROCESS OF REPENTANCE

To repent, we must follow the five Rs:

1. Recognize that we are doing wrong.
2. Regret or have remorse for the wrongdoing.
3. Resolve to live the Savior's teachings.
4. Reform our lives and refrain from doing the offensive acts again.
5. To the extent possible, make restitution for the wrongs we have done.

Paul in 2 Corinthians 7:9–10 stated, "I rejoice, not that ye were made sorry, but that ye sorrowed to repentance: for ye were made sorry after a godly manner, that ye might receive damage by us in nothing. For godly sorrow worketh repentance to salvation not to be repented of: but the sorrow of the world worketh death." This "godly sorrow" is a sorrow based upon faith and the love we have for Jesus Christ. The basis of faith is love. The basis of repentance is faith in the hope of forgiveness.

Remember, John the Baptist's mission was to declare Christ and repentance to the people: "In those days came John the Baptist, preaching in the wilderness of Judaea, and saying, Repent ye: for the kingdom of heaven is at hand" (Matthew 3:1–2).

After Jesus' forty-day fast, "from that time Jesus began to preach, and to say, Repent: for the kingdom of heaven is at hand" (Matthew 4:17).

When Jesus "sat at meat" with publicans and sinners, the Pharisees said to his disciples, "Why eateth your Master with publicans and sinners?" Jesus heard this and said to them, "They that be whole need not a physician, but they that are sick. But go ye and learn what that meaneth, I will have mercy, and not sacrifice: for I am not come to call the righteous, but sinners to repentance" (Matthew 9:10–13).

Christ on another occasion said, "Except ye repent, ye shall . . . perish" (Luke 13:3).

John the Beloved wrote: "If we say that we have no sin, we deceive ourselves, and the truth is not in us. If we confess our sins, he is faithful and just to forgive us our sins, and to cleanse us from all unrighteousness. If we say that we have not sinned, we make him a liar, and his word is not in us" (1 John 1:8–10). We all have sinned and come short of the glory of God. Yet God provides us a way out—a way of overcoming our sins through repentance.

In Luke 15 are a number of parables ending with the parable of the prodigal son, who sinned against heaven and his father. The rehabilitation of the prodigal son shows that the Lord will accept our sincere repentance and give us bountiful blessings if we repent and live the gospel.

CHRIST IS THE PROPITIATION OF OUR SINS

We must always remember that repentance is possible only because Christ came to earth as our Redeemer: "And he is the propitiation for our sins: and not for ours only, but also for the sins of the whole world" (1 John 2:2). We read in 1 John 4:10, "Herein is love, not that we loved God, but that he loved us, and sent his Son to be the propitiation for our sins." In Romans 3:25, we read that God has sent Christ "to be a propitiation through faith in his blood, to declare his righteousness for the remission of sins that are past, through the forbearance of God."

Repentance is a gift from God—a pardon from God, which he will liberally give us as we go through the process of repentance. It is a great gift when we consider that not one of us is perfect. We are all subject to the weaknesses of the flesh. That is why we need the Savior.

CHAPTER 10

BAPTISM

Infants are not barred from the Kingdom of Heaven just because they happen to depart the present life before they have been immersed in water.

—JOHN CALVIN

FAITH AND REPENTANCE are the first two principles of the gospel. Baptism is the first ordinance of the gospel. Various churches have various forms of baptism, such as dipping, pouring, sprinkling, forward immersion, backward immersion, trine immersion, rose petals, dirt, and sand. Yet Mormons rightly believe, and the Bible teaches, that there is only one correct form of baptism: immersion by one having the authority or priesthood of God to baptize. Baptism is an absolutely essential ordinance if we are to enter the kingdom of God.

What about the various forms of baptism? Paul stated in Ephesians 4:5 that there is "one Lord, one faith, one baptism." Galatians 3:27 says, "As many of you as have been baptized into Christ have put on Christ."

We accept Christ by being baptized. Baptism is a saving ordinance. We will never understand the Atonement of Christ as our individual release from sin unless we are baptized.

In John 3:3–5 we read, "Jesus answered and said unto [Nicodemus], Verily, verily, I say unto thee, Except a man be born again, he cannot see the kingdom of God. Nicodemus saith unto him, How can a man be born when he is old? can he enter the second time into his mother's womb, and be born? Jesus answered, Verily, verily, I say unto thee, Except a man be born of water and of the Spirit, he cannot enter into the kingdom of God."

Peter said, "Repent, and be baptized every one of you in the name of Jesus Christ for the remission of sins, and ye shall receive the gift of the Holy Ghost" (Acts 2:38).

In Mark 16:16 the Savior said, "He that believeth and is baptized shall be saved."

Luke, emphasizing the importance of baptism, said, "The Pharisees and lawyers rejected the counsel of God against themselves, being not baptized of him" (Luke 7:30).

Paul (then named Saul) was one who persecuted the early Christians. While on the way to Damascus, he had a powerful vision. He fell to the ground and heard a voice saying, "Saul, Saul, why persecutest thou me?" He answered, "Who art thou, Lord?" Christ said unto him, "I am Jesus of Nazareth, whom thou persecutest." What did Paul do? He immediately responded: "What shall I do, Lord?" (Acts 22:7–10)

He was told to go into Damascus where he would receive further instructions. In Acts 22:16 we learn what he was to do. "Why tarriest thou? arise, and be baptized, and wash away thy sins, calling on the name of the Lord." Even Paul, one of the greatest witnesses of Christ, had to be baptized.

The Bible is clear that we must be baptized in order to enter the kingdom of God. If it was necessary for Christ to be baptized, in the fulfillment of all righteousness, then it is even more necessary for us to be baptized. Christ's admonition to his apostles was, "Go ye . . . and teach all nations, baptizing them in the name of the Father, and of the Son, and of the Holy Ghost" (Matthew 28:19). He also said in Mark 16:15–16, "Go ye into all the world, and preach the gospel to every creature. He that believeth and is baptized shall be saved; but he that believeth not shall be damned."

The purpose of baptism is explained in Mark 1:4: "John did baptize in the wilderness, and preach the baptism of repentance for the remission of sins." Luke 3:3 says, "He came into all the country about Jordan, preaching the baptism of repentance for the remission of sins."

THE FORM OF BAPTISM

If there is only "one Lord, one faith, one baptism," what should be the form of baptism? The verb baptize comes from the Greek *bapto, baptizo,* and literally means "to dip" or "to immerse."

Paul wrote in Romans 6:3–5: "Know ye not, that so many of us as were baptized into Jesus Christ were baptized into his death? Therefore we are *buried* with him by baptism into death: that like as Christ was raised up from the dead by the glory of the Father, even so we also should walk in newness of life. For if we have been *planted* together in the likeness of his death, we shall be also in the likeness of his resurrection." Here Paul refers to baptism as being "buried" or "planted." We must conclude that we must be immersed under the water to meet the form of baptism Paul referred to as the "one baptism" (Ephesians 4:5).

The Greeks understand baptism to mean burial in water. In fact, ancient writers like Polybius, a historian of the second century, spoke of the naval battle between the Carthaginian and Roman fleets off the shores of Sicily: "If any were hard pressed by the enemy they withdrew safely back, on account of their fast sailing, into the open sea, and then turning around and falling on those of their pursuers who were in advance, they gave them frequent blows and *baptized* many of their vessels" (Polybius, book 1, chapter 51).

For more than two centuries after the Savior's resurrection, immersion was the Christian mode of baptism. This changed at the end of the third century when the ordinance was distorted.

But Christ set the example for all of us, as described in Matthew 3:16: "Jesus, when he was baptized, went up straightway out of the water." Clearly, he was baptized by immersion.

See also Acts 8:35–39, where Philip baptized the eunuch: "Philip opened his mouth, and began at the same scripture, and preached unto him Jesus. And as they went on their way, they came unto a certain water: and the eunuch said, See, here is water; what doth hinder me to be baptized? And Philip said, If thou believest with all thine heart, thou mayest. And he answered and said, I believe that Jesus Christ is the Son of God. And he commanded the chariot to stand still: *and they went down both into the water,* both Philip and the eunuch; and he baptized him. And *when they were come up out of the water,* the Spirit of the Lord caught away Philip, that the eunuch saw him no more: and he went on his way rejoicing."

John 3:23 states, "John . . . was baptizing in Ænon near to Salim, because there was much water there: and they came, and were baptized." Why would John choose a place of "much water" unless he was baptizing by immersion?

Ancient history and archaeology prove that the early Christian baptisms were by immersion. In fact, a number of ancient Christian baptismal fonts have been discovered. Clearly, immersion is the correct form of baptism.

AUTHORITY NEEDED TO PERFORM BAPTISMS

If one form of baptism is important, then isn't it even more important to determine who can perform baptisms in the name of the Father, Son, and Holy Ghost? (Matthew 28:19) Certainly, the person performing such baptisms must hold the authority or priesthood of God in order to do so. (See chapter 12 on priesthood authority.)

INFANT BAPTISM

All of us have met young couples who have lost a child in infancy. One couple expressed tremendous anguish and concern that their deceased infant had not been baptized. They questioned aloud whether the child could go to heaven. The worry and fear was eating the life out of the mother. Losing the child was bad enough, but would this beloved infant be forever lost from God and his influence?

What about little children? Do they need to be baptized, or do only persons who are accountable need baptism? Mark 10:13–16 shows that little children do not need to be baptized: "They brought young children to him, that he should touch them: and his disciples rebuked those that brought them. But when Jesus saw it, he was much displeased, and said unto them, Suffer the little children to come unto me, and forbid them not: for of such is the kingdom of God. Verily I say unto you, Whosoever shall not receive the kingdom of God as a little child, he shall not enter therein. And he took them up in his arms, put his hands upon them, and blessed them."

From these scriptures, it is difficult for anyone to conclude that little children will not be saved. I have already quoted Mark 16:16, which says, "He that believeth and is baptized shall be saved; but he that believeth not shall be damned." One must be accountable in order to believe. Little children are not accountable until they can rationally make choices. Many psychologists say children have this accountability at approximately eight years of age.

The Book of Mormon is particularly explicit concerning little children: "Listen to the words of Christ, your Redeemer, your Lord and your God. Behold, I came into the world not to call the righteous but sinners to repentance; the whole need no physician, but they that are sick; wherefore, little children are whole, for they are not capable of committing sin; wherefore the curse of Adam is taken from them in me, that it hath no power over them; and the law of circumcision is done away in me. And after this manner did the Holy Ghost manifest the word of God unto me; wherefore, my beloved son, I know that it is solemn mockery before God, that ye should baptize little children. Behold I say unto you that this thing shall ye teach—repentance and baptism unto those who are accountable and capable of committing sin; yea, teach parents that they must repent and be baptized, and humble themselves as their little children, and they shall all be saved with their little children. And their little children need no repentance, neither baptism. Behold, baptism is unto repentance to the fulfilling the commandments unto the remission of sins. But little children are alive in Christ, even from the foundation of the world; if not so, God is a partial God, and also a changeable God, and a respecter to persons; for how many little children have died without baptism! Wherefore, if little children could not be saved without baptism, these must have gone to an endless hell. Behold I say unto you, that he that supposeth that little children need baptism is in the gall of bitterness and in the bonds of iniquity; for he hath neither faith, hope, nor charity; wherefore, should he be cut off while in the thought, he must go down to hell. For awful is the wickedness to suppose that God saveth one child because of baptism, and the other must perish because he hath no baptism" (Moroni 8:8–15).

Before the devout gentile Cornelius was baptized, Peter, a Jew, had to accept the revelation that Gentiles were acceptable to God. When Peter did acknowledge that fact, he exclaimed, "Of a truth I perceive that God is no respecter of persons: but in every nation he that feareth him, and worketh righteousness, is accepted with him" (Acts 10:34–35).

One must "fear" God, work righteousness, and be baptized in order to be accepted by God. Clearly little children, especially infants who die before the age of accountability, are too young to "believe," "fear" God, or work righteousness. If they die in infancy, they are saved in the kingdom of God in spite of the teachings of some who say they will go to purgatory or be lost from heaven.

CHAPTER 11

THE HOLY GHOST

Then laid they their hands on them, and they received the Holy Ghost.

—ACTS 8:17

BAPTISM is the first ordinance of the gospel. The second ordinance of the gospel is the laying on of hands for the gift of the Holy Ghost. Remember Matthew 3:16–17: "Jesus, when he was baptized, went up straightway out of the water: and, lo, the heavens were opened unto him, and he saw the Spirit of God descending like a dove, and lighting upon him."

In Matthew 3:11 John the Baptist made it clear that "he that cometh after me is mightier than I, whose shoes I am not worthy to bear: he shall baptize you with the Holy Ghost, and with fire." He was clearly foretelling the coming of Christ, who would bring with him the power to lay on hands for the gift of the Holy Ghost.

In Acts 8:14–20, the gospel had been preached in Samaria, and a number of people had been baptized. However, none of them had received the Holy Ghost. The apostles heard that they "had received the word of God" and sent Peter and John to give these new converts the Holy Ghost: "Then laid they their hands on them, and they received the Holy Ghost."

In Acts 19:1–6, Paul came to Ephesus and found certain believers in Jesus Christ. He naturally asked them, "Have ye received the Holy Ghost since ye believed?" They answered him, "We have not so much as heard whether there be any Holy Ghost." Paul, surprised, and knowing that true ministers always promised the Holy Ghost after baptism, asked them, "Unto what then were ye baptized?" They responded, "Unto John's baptism." In other words, they had been baptized by immersion, as John performed baptisms, but they had never heard of the Holy Ghost. Apparently, they were sincere in their beliefs and their actions. A sincere minister probably baptized them, but he could not have had the authority of God because he didn't tell them about the necessity of being baptized with "fire and the Holy Ghost." No true minister would have failed to preach that doctrine. Paul told them that "John verily baptized with the baptism of repentance, saying unto the people, that they should believe on him which should come after him, that is, on Christ Jesus." Therefore, they had to be rebaptized: "When they heard this, they were baptized in the name of the Lord Jesus. And when Paul *had laid his hands upon them, the Holy Ghost came on them*."

Paul understood that the minister who baptized them could not have held the priesthood because he did not even know of the Holy Ghost. Therefore, when Paul explained the importance of the Holy Ghost, these sincere believers knew they had to be rebaptized by Paul, who held the priesthood.

Hebrews 6:2–4 mentions the "doctrine of baptisms, and of *laying on of hands*" and then speaks of "those who were once enlightened, and have tasted of the heavenly gift, and were made partakers of the Holy Ghost." The conferring of the Holy Ghost is an important part of the gospel of Jesus Christ. The reception of the Holy Ghost is a requisite for those who want to understand the gospel.

The Holy Ghost is called the "Spirit of truth" and the "Comforter" who will "teach you all things, and bring all things to your remembrance, whatsoever I have said unto you" (John 14:17, 26).

In John 16:13, Jesus explained, "When he, the Spirit of truth, is come, he will guide you into all truth: for he shall not speak of himself; but whatsoever he shall hear, that shall he speak: and he will shew you things to come."

In John 15:26 Christ said, "When the Comforter is come, whom I will send unto you from the Father, even the Spirit of truth, which proceedeth from the Father, *he shall testify of me*."

In Luke 12:12, Jesus taught, "The Holy Ghost shall teach you . . . what ye ought to say."

Paul explains in Romans 8:16, "The Spirit itself beareth witness with our spirit, that we are the children of God."

There is no question that we can be influenced by the Holy Ghost before we are baptized. He can and does bear testimony to us of the divinity of Jesus Christ. However, the scriptures tell us that we must accept his teachings and then live them for the Holy Ghost to stay with us and guide us.

Acts 5:32 states, "We are his witnesses of these things; and so is also the Holy Ghost, *whom God hath given to them that obey him.*" To continue to enjoy the influence of the Holy Ghost, once we know the truth, we must "obey him" and live God's teachings, including faith, repentance, and baptism. If we do not, we endanger our right to have the Holy Ghost remain with us to protect and inspire us.

There is another aspect to Acts 5:32. We may have a miraculous manifestation of the Spirit to help us find the truth. Yet, if we do not accept the gospel, have faith, repent, be baptized, and receive the Holy Ghost through the administration of those in authority, we will not have obeyed him. (See chapter 12 on priesthood authority.) Regardless of our profound manifestation, unless we obey, the Holy Ghost will leave us.

These first principles (faith and repentance) and ordinances (baptism and the laying on of hands for the gift of the Holy Ghost) are part of what we committed to live when we shouted for joy at the prospect of coming to the earth to gain a body and become more like God. We must now live worthy of returning to God's presence.

CHAPTER 12

PRIESTHOOD AUTHORITY

Ye have not chosen me, but I have chosen you, and ordained you.

—JESUS TO HIS APOSTLES (JOHN 15:16)

WE ALL FACE the problem of determining what is right. When we speak of the authority to act for God, we refer to the priesthood of God. We cannot imagine God sanctioning as his own eight hundred different Christian churches, each teaching different doctrines, each contradicting the others, each claiming to be the one true church. Surely when Paul, as one of the apostles, spoke of one Lord, one faith, and one baptism (Ephesians 4:5), he was speaking for Christ.

But which of all of these churches, each claiming to act for God, is right? Which has the true baptism and the true authority to baptize? How do we find this one true church?

The one true church has the priesthood or power of God to perform his ordinances. It teaches the truth about the Godhead and has the answers to the great questions of life.

Think about it. These are true and eternal principles. God gives authority only to those who act in his name.

The authority—the priesthood—is, among other things, essential to administer the ordinances of baptism and the laying on of hands for the gift of the Holy Ghost.

Christ was the only perfect person (Hebrews 5:9) ever to live on the earth. As the perfect Son of God, Christ must have been perfect in his activities, especially in his establishment of his church. Therefore, his church must also have been perfectly organized. If that perfectly organized and established church was necessary then, it must be equally necessary today.

CHRIST CHOSE TWELVE APOSTLES AS THE FOUNDATION OF HIS CHURCH

One of the first things Christ did was to choose twelve apostles from among all of his disciples, or followers.

In John 15:16 Jesus told these apostles, "Ye have not chosen me, but I have chosen you, *and ordained you*, that ye should go and bring forth fruit [converts], and that your fruit should remain: that whatsoever ye shall ask of the Father in my name, he may give it you."

These apostles did not choose the Savior. He chose them and ordained them to the priesthood. He gave them the authority to act for him after he left the earth.

In fact, Christ told his apostles in Matthew 16:19, "I will give unto thee the keys of the kingdom of heaven: and whatsoever thou shalt bind on earth shall be bound in heaven: and whatsoever thou shalt loose on earth shall be loosed in heaven." This must be an awesome power.

Mark 3:14–15 explains, "He ordained twelve, that they should be with him, and that he might send them forth to preach, and to have power to heal sicknesses, and to cast out devils."

Matthew 10:5–8 states: "These twelve Jesus sent forth, and commanded them, saying, Go not into the way of the Gentiles, and into any city of the Samaritans enter ye not: but go rather to the lost sheep of the house of Israel. And as ye go, preach, saying, The kingdom of heaven is at hand. Heal the sick, cleanse the lepers, raise the dead, cast out devils: freely ye have received, freely give."

These apostles were the foundation of the Church (Ephesians 2:19–21).

CHRIST'S CHURCH—A PERFECT ORGANIZATION

Paul, writing powerfully to the Ephesians (newly baptized members of the Church), in Ephesians 2:19–21 said, "Now . . . *ye are no more strangers and foreigners, but fellowcitizens with the saints* [members of the Church], and of the household of God; and *are built upon the foundation of the apostles and prophets*, Jesus Christ himself being the chief corner stone; in whom all the building fitly framed together groweth unto an holy temple in the Lord."

These newly baptized members of the Church had become fellowcitizens with the Saints; in other words, they had become members of the Church themselves. That's all the word *saints* meant in New Testament times: members of the church of Jesus Christ.

More significantly, the Church had as its foundation apostles and prophets.

If we have the Church of Jesus Christ today, shouldn't it have as its foundation apostles and prophets? Yes! Christ made it clear that the Church needed apostles and prophets as he filled the vacant positions of the Quorum of the Twelve Apostles each time an apostle died. (See Acts 1:22–26, where Matthias was chosen to replace Judas.)

The scriptures clearly state, "He gave some, apostles; and some, prophets; and some, evangelists; and some, pastors and teachers; for the perfecting of the saints, for the work of the ministry, for the edifying of the body of Christ [the Church]: till we all come in the unity of the faith, and of the knowledge of the Son of God, unto a perfect man, unto the measure of the stature of the fulness of Christ: that we henceforth be no more children, tossed to and fro, and carried about with every wind of doctrine by the sleight of men, and cunning craftiness, whereby they lie in wait to deceive" (Ephesians 4:11–14). Here we have five of the eleven offices Christ filled through ordination to carry on the work of the ministry of his Church.

Actually, according to the scriptures, Christ ordained leaders to eleven different offices in his church for (1) "the perfecting of the saints" (members of the Church), (2) "the work of the ministry," (3) "for the edifying of the body of Christ" or the Church members, and (4) "till we all come in the unity of the faith, and of the knowledge of the Son of God."

If we are doing the "work of the ministry" and edifying the body of Christ, or the Church, we must have these offices of the priesthood to assist us. We need this perfect organization of eleven offices in the priesthood "till we all come in the unity of the faith." Those who profess Christianity are no more near a unity of the faith today than we ever were. Therefore, we still need this perfect organization of ordained priesthood workers organized exactly as Christ set it up.

Other offices were also important in Christ's church anciently, for the apostles "ordained . . . elders in every church, and . . . commended them to the Lord, on whom they believed" (Acts 14:23). Actually, they ordained deacons, teachers, priests, elders, seventies, high priests, bishops, pastors, and evangelists to help with the work of the ministry, as mentioned in the following verses:

Apostles and prophets: Ephesians 4:11

Evangelists: Ephesians 4:11; 2 Timothy 4:5

Pastors: Ephesians 4:11

Teachers: Ephesians 4:11; 1 Corinthians 12:28–29

Deacons: Philippians 1:1

Priests: Acts 6:7

Elders: Acts 14:23; Titus 1:5; James 5:14

Seventies: Luke 10:1, 17

High priests: Hebrews 3:1; 5:10; 6:20; 7:26

Bishops: Philippians 1:1; 1 Timothy 3:1–7

Clearly, Jesus Christ, the perfect man, established a perfect organization that he called his church.

A church is not a building but the organization through which the gospel is preached and those in authority perform the ordinances. Because Christ was perfect, he established a perfect and necessary church organization. If Christ's church was perfect or necessary then, it must also be perfect and necessary today. It is logical, then, that the true church of Jesus Christ would have the same organization today, with deacons, teachers, priests, elders, seventies, high priests, bishops, pastors, evangelists, apostles, and prophets. Through revelation, The Church of Jesus Christ of Latter-day Saints (the Mormon Church) is organized exactly the same as the church Christ set up anciently. In these latter days, it is the only church with this perfect priesthood organization.

CHRIST'S UNPAID LAY MINISTRY

Many years ago in Pittsburgh, Pennsylvania, I was asked to represent my church at a huge convocation of tri-state ministers. Since seats were not assigned at the luncheon, I tried to pick a table at which a number of different religions were represented. I found the perfect table where, if I recall correctly, two Catholic priests (one a Maronist father who had taken a vow of poverty), a Presbyterian minister, a Baptist minister, an Episcopalian rector, and a few others were seated.

I asked if I could take the empty seat. The Episcopalian rector asked me, "What religion do you represent?"

I replied, "I'm an elder in the Mormon Church."

"We don't want you," he retorted with a smile.

I laughed, and as I took my seat I replied, "Small wonder; our Mormon missionaries are converting more than ten thousand of your parishioners in England every year."

Everyone laughed, and they accepted me with friendship and kindness.

During the luncheon, the conversation became serious when one of the ministers noted sadly that young people are not coming into the ministry as they did in times past.

I asked, "Why do you think that is?"

One of the ministers responded, "Well, in times past, the local minister was the most relied upon and respected person in the community. When people had problems, they went to him. When troubles arose, he became the arbiter who helped solve them. However, in our complex times, there is not the same prestige or incentives in becoming a minister."

Another minister stated that the ministers of today are overworked and underappreciated. It used to be that they could spend most of the week preparing for their sermons on Sunday. Today, however, many people expect their ministers to have the answers to every problem. Thus, the demands are overwhelming. He said that the rewards of the ministry do not overcome the unappreciated overly hard work it entails.

Yet another minister said the demands on the clergy are so exhausting and the remuneration so slight that young people are not interested in going into the ministry. They simply are not paid enough to justify the eighty-hour weeks their parishioners expect of them. There are more lucrative and more fulfilling opportunities for the young altruists of today.

At that point, I said, "Please allow me to give a few reasons why young people are not going into the ministry today."

The others looked at me as though they were thinking, "What could this lay elder in the Mormon Church possibly add to this discussion?"

I continued, "I can think of two reasons why young people are not excited to go into the ministry today: first, because ministers today are not teaching the gospel of Jesus Christ, and second, because ministers are being paid to preach the gospel."

The rector sniffed at me. "What do you mean, Mr. Hatch?"

"Let me ask you a question," I said. "How much did Christ pay his apostles and prophets to teach his gospel?"

There were puzzled looks all around. Finally, someone said, "Nothing."

I replied, "Oh, he paid them all right, but not in money. They were paid in special blessings."

Everyone agreed, although some of them looked at me suspiciously, wondering where I was about to take them.

I then asked, "How many of you, if your salaries were cut off today, would be at the pulpit next Sunday?" A number of hands went up. "Two months from now?" Only two hands went up. "What about a year from now?" No hands were raised, and everyone was looking quite pensive.

One of the ministers exclaimed, "But what would we do for a living?"

I responded, "What did Christ's ministers do for a living?"

Someone said, "Paul was a tentmaker."

"That's right," I responded. I then quoted Matthew 10:5–8: "These twelve Jesus sent forth, and commanded them, saying, Go not into the way of the Gentiles, and into any city of the Samaritans enter ye not: but go rather to the lost sheep of the house of Israel. And as ye go, preach, saying, The kingdom of heaven is at hand. Heal the sick, cleanse the lepers, raise the dead, cast out devils: *freely ye have received, freely give.*"

I continued, "Paul, when confronted with the same problem, replied, 'What is my reward then? Verily that, which I preach the gospel, *I may make the gospel of Christ without charge*, that I *abuse not my power in the gospel*'" (1 Corinthians 9:18).

The Maronist priest was enjoying the discussion because he had taken a vow of poverty.

I then quoted from memory Christ's lucid statements in John 10:11–13: "I am the good shepherd: the good shepherd giveth his life for the sheep. But he that is an hireling, and not the shepherd, whose own the sheep are not, seeth the wolf coming, and leaveth the sheep, and fleeth: and the wolf catcheth them, and scattereth the sheep. *The hireling fleeth, because he is an hireling, and careth not for the sheep.*"

"Please understand," I said. "You are all sincere and devoted people. You raise a practical issue. How can you support your families without a ministerial salary? If you do not have the perfect organization Christ established, with deacons, teachers, priests, elders, seventies, high priests, bishops, pastors, evangelists, apostles, and prophets, the whole burden falls on you. If you have this perfect organization, then you have a great number of fellow officers in the church to share the burden so that all can give freely of their time to spread the gospel and watch over the flock. Then, when the wolf comes, in whatever form, you will not have to flee, and the flock will be spared.

"Christ made it clear that his ministry should not be a paid one because, when hard times come, his ministers will not scatter and run. They will stand and fight for the flock because they are doing the work of the Lord because of their faith, not for remuneration."

When the luncheon was over, one of the ministers said to me, "Young man, you have given us a lot to think about. I really enjoyed the discussion of the scriptures. The trouble with modern Christianity is that we don't often discuss the doctrines and the scriptures that support them."

The others, too, were friendly as they departed for their meetings.

The Church of Jesus Christ of Latter-day Saints has the only unpaid lay ministry and missionary system in the world. Because of this unpaid ministry, the Church's presiding officers do not have to do all the work of the Church themselves. Bishops, pastors, evangelists, apostles, and prophets can call upon deacons, teachers, priests, elders, seventies, and high priests to voluntarily assist them in the ministry. That is how Christ envisioned his priesthood organization.

The priesthood has been on the earth since the beginning. In Hebrews 5:4 we read, "No man taketh this honour unto himself, but he that is called of God, as was Aaron." Remember, Aaron was the brother of the prophet Moses and was called to the priesthood in the time of Moses. He held the Aaronic or lower priesthood. See Exodus 28:1–2 where Moses was told, "Take thou unto thee Aaron thy brother, and his sons with him, from among the children of Israel, that he may minister unto me in the priest's office, even Aaron, Nadab and Abihu, Eleazar and Ithamar, Aaron's sons. And thou shalt make holy garments for Aaron thy brother for glory and for beauty."

Clearly, if a man is to be called of God as was Aaron, it must be through revelation from God through his living prophet. (See Exodus 40:13–15; Numbers 25:13.)

The power of the priesthood is magnificent. In Matthew 10:1, the Lord gathered his twelve apostles and "gave them power against unclean spirits, to cast them out, and to heal all manner of sickness and all manner of disease."

In Matthew 28:18–19 we read, "Jesus came and spake unto them, saying, All power is given unto me in heaven and in earth. Go ye therefore, and teach all nations, baptizing them in the name of the Father, and of the Son, and of the Holy Ghost."

In Mark 3:14–15, Christ "ordained twelve, that they should be with him, and that he might send them forth to preach, and to have power to heal sicknesses, and to cast out devils."

In Luke 10:19, Christ gave to the seventy "power to tread on serpents and scorpions, and over all the power of the enemy."

Many of us who hold the priesthood have personally seen the lame walk, the blind see, the deaf hear, and countless other miracles as a result of blessings by those holding the priesthood in these latter days.

THE PRIESTHOOD OF GOD CANNOT BE PURCHASED

One of the great stories about the priesthood concerns Philip as he preached in Samaria. Apparently he held the Aaronic or lesser priesthood and thus had only the power to baptize with water. Like John the Baptist, he did not have the power to baptize with the "Holy Ghost, and with fire" (Matthew 3:11). He baptized the Samarians and, like John the Baptist, told them that later they would be given the Holy Ghost (Acts 8:5, 12).

"Now when the apostles which were at Jerusalem heard that

Samaria had received the word of God, they sent unto them Peter and John: Who, when they were come down, prayed for them, that they might receive the Holy Ghost: (For as yet he was fallen upon none of them: only they were baptized in the name of the Lord Jesus.) Then laid they their hands on them, and they received the Holy Ghost" (Acts 8:14–17). Peter and John, holding the higher or Melchizedek Priesthood, had the authority to convey the Holy Ghost (Hebrews 5:6; 7:11–12).

Yet there is another lesson to be learned about the priesthood in this story. There was a man called Simon (Acts 8:9) who had practiced sorcery and "bewitched" the people of Samaria. "And when Simon saw that through laying on of the apostles' hands the Holy Ghost was given, he offered them money, saying, Give me also this power, that on whomsoever I lay hands, he may receive the Holy Ghost. But Peter said unto him, Thy money perish with thee, because thou hast thought that the gift of God may be purchased with money" (Acts 8:18–20).

We must conclude that God's priesthood authority cannot be purchased.

IS SINCERITY ENOUGH?

Some have argued that God recognizes any sincere minister's baptism. That is not true. Mere sincerity is not enough.

For any baptism to be recognized by God, the officiator must hold the true priesthood of God. See Acts 19:1–6, where Paul was passing through the upper coasts and came to Ephesus, where he found certain disciples (followers). Realizing that missionaries like Philip, who held only the Aaronic Priesthood (the power to baptize but not to lay on hands for the gift of the Holy Ghost), were baptizing converts ahead of his arrival, Paul asked the disciples, "Have ye received the Holy Ghost since ye believed?" They answered, "We have not so much as heard whether there be any Holy Ghost." Here were sincere followers of Christ who had not even heard of the Holy Ghost. So Paul, recognizing their sincerity, asked them, "Unto what then were ye baptized?" They responded, "Unto John's baptism." Paul then explained, "John verily baptized with the baptism of repentance, saying unto the people, that they should believe on him which should come after him, that is, on Christ Jesus." Remember, John the Baptist always said that one would come after him who would baptize with the Holy Ghost and with fire (Matthew 3:11).

These were sincere disciples who had been baptized by immersion by an apparently sincere minister. Since the person who baptized them did not know of the Holy Ghost, that "minister" could not have held the priesthood of God. Therefore, even though a sincere minister had baptized them, they had to be rebaptized by one who actually had the authority or priesthood. "When they heard this, they were baptized in the name of the Lord Jesus. And when Paul had laid his hands upon them, the Holy Ghost came on them; and they spake with tongues, and prophesied" (Acts 19:5–6).

All the sincerity in the world will not substitute for being baptized by one who holds the true priesthood of God.

We can learn much from the Old Testament about the priesthood. One of the most important priesthood stories of the Old Testament concerned Uzzah, who stretched forth his hand to steady the Ark of the Covenant and was struck dead.

In Numbers 1:50–51, we learn of the important principle that only the true priesthood holders could be in charge of the tabernacle and handle the vessels of the tabernacle. As the Lord told Moses: "Appoint the Levites over the tabernacle of testimony, and over all the vessels thereof, and over all things that belong to it: they shall bear the tabernacle, and all the vessels thereof; and they shall minister unto it, and shall encamp round about the tabernacle. And when the tabernacle setteth forward, the Levites shall take it down: and when the tabernacle is to be pitched, the Levites shall set it up: *and the stranger that cometh nigh shall be put to death.*"

In 1 Chronicles 15:2 we read, "David said, None ought to carry the ark of God but the Levites: for them hath the Lord chosen to carry the ark of God, and to minister unto him for ever."

These scriptures set the stage for the story of Uzzah. No one but the Levites or the holders of the Levitical Priesthood [Aaronic Priesthood] could handle the ark of God, and the non-priesthood-holding stranger would die if he violated this instruction.

In the story of Uzzah, the people of David were bringing the ark of God to Jerusalem, and those who had the authority to handle it had placed it on a "new cart" (2 Samuel 6:3). "And when they came to Nachon's threshingfloor, Uzzah put forth his hand to the ark of God, and took hold of it; for the oxen shook it. *And the anger of the Lord was kindled against Uzzah; and God smote him there for his error; and there he died by the ark of God*" (2 Samuel 6:6–7).

This seems harsh, but God used this incident to impress upon the children of Israel the importance of his instructions concerning the priesthood handling the ark. The Lord expected appropriate respect to be shown for his ark and the priesthood holders who handled it.

Only priesthood holders could handle the ark of God. So isn't it as important that the Church of Christ be administered by those having the priesthood authority to do so?

The true church, which has the priesthood of God, must have the perfect organization leading it. Isn't it logical that the true church should understand the important principles of life, including knowledge of whence we came, why we are here, where we are going, the nature of the Godhead, and the first principles and ordinances of the gospel? What a blessing it is to know that those who baptize us and bestow upon us the Holy Ghost have the authority to do so.

CHAPTER 13

LOOKING FOR THE TRUE CHURCH

How be it my church save it be called in my name? For if a church be called in Moses' name then it be Moses' church; or if it be called in the name of a man then it be the church of a man; but if it be called in my name then it is my church, if it so be that they are built upon my gospel.

—3 NEPHI 27:8

TODAY THERE ARE hundreds of different churches, all teaching different doctrines—one contradicting another. Paul spoke of only one church, one faith, one baptism (Ephesians 4:5). How do we know which church we should join?

Why is it that most churches teach that the Father, Son, and Holy Ghost are all one being substance or essence—an analogy like water, steam, and ice—three different aspects of the same substance? The scriptures teach that the Father, Son, and Holy Ghost are three separate and distinct beings (Matthew 3:16–17; Acts 7:55–56).

Why do some churches teach that God is only a spirit without a body when the scriptures teach that God is a perfect being with a perfect body of flesh and bones? Remember, Christ, his Son, was raised from the dead with a body of flesh and bones united with his spirit, never to die again (Romans 6:9). Therefore, since death is the separation of the body and the spirit (James 2:26), Christ will always have his perfect, resurrected body of flesh and bones. Christ is in the express image of God's person (Hebrews 1:1–3), and he and God created man in their own image and likeness (Genesis 1:26–27). Therefore, God the Father also has a perfect body of flesh and bones united with his spirit.

Why is it that the churches of today, as sincere as each is, do not have a full knowledge and understanding of the premortal existence and the fact that we are all spirit children of God the Eternal Father?

Why is it that the churches of today do not understand the antiquity of the gospel—that the gospel has been on the earth since the beginning, although it has been taken away from time to time?

This is an eternal truth. We knew of the gospel in the premortal existence, and Adam knew about it at the time of his earth life. Successive prophets have also had knowledge of the gospel right down to the time of Christ. (See 1 Corinthians 10:1–4; Galatians 3:8; Hebrews 4:2,6; 11:26–27.)

Why is it the churches of today do not have apostles and prophets as their foundation? (Ephesians 2:19–21). If they were necessary as the foundation of the Church in the meridian of time, why not now? Ephesians 4:11–14 tells us they are necessary for the perfecting of the members of Christ's church, for the edification of the members of the Church, for the work of the ministry and the preaching of the gospel until we all come to a unity of the faith. They are also necessary to receive the requisite revelation to solve the distinct problems of our own modern times.

If we must have apostles and prophets to guide the true church in righteousness, then where are they? If they are here, how did they get here? Who gave them the authority? How might we know them? What role did they play in the restoration of the gospel? Are they truly the foundation of the Church of Christ? Is the rest of the Church "fitly framed" with all the other officers Christ established in the Church in the meridian of time? (Ephesians 2:19–21; 4:11–14).

Why is it that churches today do not claim revelation from God to guide us in these modern times? Since God raised up prophets to guide us through all dispensations of time, why not now? Remember, after Christ left the earth, he gave "commandments unto the apostles whom he had chosen" (Acts 1:2). Since the churches are living without God's continual involvement and advice, we have a lack of consistent perspective. Are some of these religions not seeking the Lord but walking in their own way?

Why is it that none of the other Christian churches have the perfect organization that Christ established consisting of deacons, teachers, priests, elders, seventies, high priests, bishops, pastors, evangelists, apostles, and prophets? (See Ephesians 2:19–21; 4:11–14.)

Isaiah, speaking of the last days said, "The earth also is defiled under the inhabitants thereof; because they have transgressed the laws, changed the ordinance, broken the everlasting covenant. Therefore hath the curse devoured the earth, and they that dwell therein are desolate: therefore the inhabitants of the earth are burned, and few men left" (Isaiah 24:5–6).

It takes little imagination to conclude that Isaiah was talking about our times, the last days, before the second coming of Christ, when the earth will be cleansed by fire. Yet here, in these verses, Isaiah makes clear that in the last days people will have fallen away from the true gospel. They will transgress the laws of God, change the ordinances of the gospel, and break the everlasting covenant of living God's principles.

In fact, in Isaiah 29:13–14, again speaking of the latter days— our time—Isaiah says, "Wherefore the Lord said, Forasmuch as this people draw near me with their mouth, and with their lips do honour me, but have removed their heart far from me, and their fear toward me is taught by the precept of men: Therefore, behold, I will proceed to do a marvellous work among this people, even a marvellous work and a wonder: for the wisdom of their wise men shall perish, and the understanding of their prudent men shall be hid."

These verses indicate that, in the last days, the world will be in a state of apostasy, and that a marvelous work and a wonder will occur to redeem the world.

THE APOSTASY AFTER CHRIST AND HIS APOSTLES LEFT THE EARTH

In Acts 20:29–30, the Apostle Paul prophesied: "I know this, that after my departing shall grievous wolves enter in among you, not sparing the flock. Also of your own selves shall men arise, speaking perverse things, to draw away disciples after them." Paul made it clear that evil men will rise up and preach apostasy so that the flock (the church) will not be spared. If something is not spared, it will no longer exist. In other words, Paul was predicting an apostasy from the true religion shortly after the death of the apostles, when the gospel would be taken from the earth. He was predicting the Dark Ages.

In Galatians 1:6, Paul marveled, "Ye are so soon removed from him that called you into the grace of Christ unto another gospel." He was amazed that the people of his day were beginning to apostatize from the truth so shortly after the death of the Savior.

In an even more explicit passage, Paul talked about the "falling away" or apostasy in stark terms. He wrote in 2 Thessalonians 2:1–3: "We beseech you, brethren, by the coming of our Lord Jesus Christ, and by our gathering together unto him, That ye be not soon shaken in mind, or be troubled, neither by spirit, nor by word, nor by letter as from us, as that the day of Christ [the second coming of Christ] is at hand. Let no man deceive you by any means: for that day shall not come, except there come a falling away first, and that man of sin be revealed, the son of perdition [the devil]."

Paul made it abundantly clear that there will be an apostasy and that Satan will take over for a time before the second coming of the Savior.

The pervasive influence of Satan during the Dark Ages is confirmed in John's prophecy in Revelation 13:7: "It was given unto him [Satan] to make war with the saints [the members of Christ's church], and to overcome them: and power was given him over all kindreds, and tongues, and nations."

This verse says that Satan would overcome the Saints. I submit that if the power of the priesthood (God's power) was on the earth at the time, the Church would have been spared (Acts 20:29) and the Saints would not have been "overcome." Put another way, if only one holder of God's priesthood had been on the earth, since God's power or priesthood is more powerful than Satan, the Church would have been spared.

We must conclude that the priesthood (the power to act for God on the earth) was taken from the earth shortly after the apostles were killed.

In fact, in AD 325, none other than Constantine, then a pagan, called the Council of Nicea to unify the Roman Empire. It was at this conference that the doctrinal change in the definition of the

Godhead occurred. Through public debate, the council decided that God, Christ, and the Holy Ghost were only one being and that this being was only a spirit without a body. It is easy to understand why Paul, approximately 260 years earlier, was amazed that the people had already begun to apostatize (Galatians 1:6–9).

There are several scriptures that foretell the apostasy from the true church. (See 1 Timothy 4:1–3; 2 Timothy 3:1–5; 4:2–4; and 2 Peter 2:1–3.)

THE PROPHESIED RESTORATION OF THE GOSPEL

One of the most important scriptures that makes the transition from the meridian of time, the time of Christ, to the modern age is Acts 3:19–21. Peter, on the day of Pentecost stated: "Repent ye . . . and be converted, that your sins may be blotted out, when the times of refreshing shall come from the presence of the Lord; and he shall send Jesus Christ, which before was preached unto you: whom the heaven must receive *until the times of restitution of all things*, which God hath spoken by the mouth of all his holy prophets since the world began."

This passage shows that the apostasy will take place before the second coming of Christ. Peter tells us to repent and be converted because the "times of refreshing shall come from the presence of the Lord." (Peter is predicting Christ's second coming.) Yet those times cannot come, and Christ must be received in heaven "until the times of restitution [restoration] of all things" which God has spoken by the mouth of all the holy prophets since the beginning of the world. If all things have to be restored, then all things must have been taken away during the time of the apostasy (the Dark Ages).

What are these "times of refreshing" or "times of restitution of all things" spoken of by Peter?

In Ephesians 1:9–10, Paul describes these "times" in terms of the last days: "Having made known unto us the mystery of his will, according to his good pleasure which he hath purposed in himself: *That in the dispensation of the fulness of times* he might gather together in one all things in Christ, both which are in heaven, and which are on earth; even in him." Here Paul describes the "times of restitution of all things" (Acts 3:21) as a time when Christ "might gather together in one all things in Christ." More specifically, he describes that period as the "dispensation of the fulness of times."

We are living in the "dispensation of the fulness of times." It is a time of restoration of all things through modern-day prophets who have been called of God to guide us in our own modern times.

Isaiah 2:2–3 says, "It shall come to pass in the last days, that the mountain of the Lord's house shall be established in the top of the mountains, and shall be exalted above the hills; and all nations shall flow unto it. And many people shall go and say, Come ye, and let us go up to the mountain of the Lord, to the house of the God of Jacob; and he will teach us of his ways, and we will walk in his paths: for out of Zion shall go forth the law, and the word of the Lord from Jerusalem." In the last days, the Lord's "house" will be established in the top of the mountains. There will be a Zion and a Jerusalem out of which the Lord's law and word will be given.

Isaiah in the foregoing scriptures foretold our times (the latter days). This prophecy is now being fulfilled, because the Lord's temple (mountain of the Lord's house) has been established in the top of the Rocky Mountains and people from all over the world are flowing unto it. As the scriptures have predicted, Israel is now reborn, and we are anxiously awaiting the second coming of the Lord.

In Daniel 2:31–44, Daniel interpreted Nebuchadnezzar's dream about the various nations that would arise from Daniel's time forward, ending in verse 44, where he clearly prophesies about the last days: "In the days of these kings shall the God of heaven set up a kingdom, which shall never be destroyed: *and the kingdom shall not be left to other people*, but it shall break in pieces and consume all these kingdoms, and it shall stand forever."

Daniel referred to this day and age when God's kingdom or church would be established, never to be destroyed again by apostasy or otherwise. It will stand forever. Thus, this must refer to the kingdom to be set up by God in the last days or the Dispensation of the Fulness of Times. Some have interpreted this kingdom mentioned in Daniel to mean the church set up by Christ in the meridian of time. Yet note in Daniel 2:44 that "the kingdom shall not be left to other people." Christ's kingdom was left to other people, as clearly stated in Matthew 21:43, where the Savior said, rebuking the Jews and those of that generation, "The kingdom of God shall be taken from you, and given to a nation bringing forth the fruit thereof." Thus, in Daniel 2:44, we see that Christ was referring to a kingdom of God in the future, not the kingdom of God Christ set up in approximately AD 34.

In Revelation 14:6, John the Beloved "saw another angel fly in the midst of heaven, having the everlasting gospel to preach unto them that dwell on the earth, and to every nation, and kindred, and tongue, and people." I testify to you that this angel has come and brought the gospel record about which John refers. We will discuss this prophecy later.

In Malachi 4:5–6, God tells us he would "send . . . Elijah the prophet before the coming of the great and dreadful day of the Lord" to turn our hearts to our forefathers. This has happened and will be discussed later in this book.

It is apparent that an apostasy from the divine church occurred after the death of the apostles and that the true church had to be restored–the restitution of all things–before Christ would come again (Acts 3:19–21). The last dispensation is biblically called the Dispensation of the Fulness of Times (Ephesians 1:9–10).

We are living in that dispensation. True prophets are presently living on the earth.

CHAPTER 14

LATTER-DAY PROPHETS

Current revelation is equally plain with that of former days in predicting the yet future manifestations of God through His appointed channels. The canon of scripture is still open; many lines, many precepts, are yet to be added.

—James E. Talmage

The prophets are the interpreters of God.

—Philo

I ONCE BROACHED the subject of prophets to a woman in Indiana, bearing my testimony that we have prophets on the earth today. She responded: "That can't be. We cannot have prophets beyond the Bible." Having remembered the logic of one of the latter-day apostles, Hugh B. Brown, I asked her, "Why?"

She exclaimed, "My minister said that we cannot have revelation in this day and age. He has a doctorate of divinity and is the most intelligent man of religion I have ever known. God cannot speak to us today. The heavens are sealed."

I told her, "I can think of only three reasons why God would not give us revelation today to solve our modern problems, since he has raised up prophets in each of the past dispensations to help people with their problems."

She agreed to listen.

"Since God has spoken to all dispensations in the past, the reason he will not speak to our dispensation in modern times is that he does not love us as much as he loved past generations."

"Oh, God is a God of love," she said. "He loves us just as much today as he loved the past generations."

"Well, that is a good argument for why there must be prophets today. Right?"

She hesitated, but she was thinking it over.

I proceeded. "Then perhaps God doesn't have the power to reveal his will to us today, although he has always done so in the past, as evidenced in the Old and New Testaments."

"Oh, God is omnipotent," she replied. "He has just as much power today as he ever had."

"Then that is another reason he would give us prophets today," I said. I continued, "I can think of only one other reason God would not reveal his will to us in these modern days. We have gained so much knowledge, sophistication, and independent thought through our higher schools of learning, including our divinity schools and seminaries—we have become so self-sufficient that we just don't need God to speak to us anymore."

The woman gasped. "We need God more today than at any other time in history!" she said. "Our problems are so great and demanding that he must be willing to speak to us today and help us with our specific and peculiar problems."

"Then what must God be doing?"

She didn't hesitate a second. "He must be revealing his will to a prophet or prophets somewhere," she admitted.

It is true. Why can't God speak to us today? Why won't he help us with our unique modern problems? If he is not a God of preferences and is "no respecter of persons" (Acts 10:34), then he must be willing to help us with our problems in this last dispensation. I testify that he is doing so through modern prophets whom he has called and authorized. The words of an ancient prophet are true: "Surely the Lord God will do nothing, but he revealeth his secret unto his servants the prophets" (Amos 3:7).

CHAPTER 15

JOSEPH SMITH THE PROPHET

Joseph Smith, the Prophet and Seer of the Lord, has done more, save Jesus only, for the salvation of men in this world, than any other man that ever lived in it.

—JOHN TAYLOR

JOSEPH SMITH, the first modern prophet, was the third son and fourth child in a family of ten children, born the 23rd day of December 1805, at Sharon, Windsor County, Vermont. He was the son of Joseph and Lucy Mack Smith. When he was ten, the family moved from Vermont to western New York, settling first at Palmyra, New York, and later in a town called Manchester.

Joseph Smith never had more than three years of formal schooling. This is significant when one considers the other chapters in this book and asks, "How is it possible that this young man, who lived only thirty-eight years, and who never had much schooling, could know so much about the scriptures as to leave us this remarkable gospel doctrine legacy?"

His family favored the Presbyterian Church, and some in the family joined it. Joseph Smith was impressed with the Methodist faith but did not belong to any organized religion. He noticed the strife, contention, differing doctrines, and contradictory religious claims among the various conflicting religions and constantly wondered, "How can they all be true when they contradict each other so much?" Naturally, he was confused.

The area in which he lived has been called the "burned-over district" because of the religious fervor there at the time. He attended revivals and other religious meetings. He wanted to belong but honestly did not know where to turn. He was only fourteen years old.

Then one day while reading in his Bible, he found these words in James 1:5–6: "If any of you lack wisdom, let him ask of God, that giveth to all men liberally, and upbraideth not; and it shall be given him. But let him ask in faith, nothing wavering. For he that wavereth is like a wave of the sea driven with the wind and tossed."

These verses were extremely powerful to young Joseph. He thought about them again and again, believing that perhaps even he, a mere boy, could talk with God in faith, and that God might respond. All he wanted to know was which church was right. He lacked wisdom. Perhaps, as James said, God would help him understand.

Joseph decided to pray alone in some nearby woods on a beautiful, clear day in the spring of 1820. His own words best describe what happened: "After I had retired to the place where I had previously designed to go, having looked around me, and finding myself alone, I kneeled down and began to offer up the desires of my heart to God. I had scarcely done so, when immediately I was seized upon by some power which entirely overcame me, and had such an astonishing influence over me as to bind my tongue so that I could not speak. Thick darkness gathered around me, and it seemed to me for a time as if I were doomed to sudden destruction.

"But, exerting all my powers to call upon God to deliver me out of the power of this enemy which had seized upon me, and at the very moment when I was ready to sink into despair and abandon myself to destruction—not to an imaginary ruin, but to the power of some actual being from the unseen world, who had such marvelous power as I had never before felt in any being—just at this moment of great alarm, I saw a pillar of light exactly over my head, above the brightness of the sun, which descended gradually until it fell upon me.

"It no sooner appeared than I found myself delivered from the enemy which held me bound. When the light rested upon me I saw two Personages, whose brightness and glory defy all description, standing above me in the air. One of them spake unto me, calling me by name and said, pointing to the other, *This is My Beloved Son. Hear Him!*

"My object in going to inquire of the Lord was to know which of all the sects was right, that I might know which to join. No sooner, therefore, did I get possession of myself, so as to be able to speak, than I asked the Personages who stood above me in the light, which of all the sects was right . . . and which I should join.

"I was answered that I must join none of them, for they were all wrong; and the Personage who addressed me said that all their creeds were an abomination in his sight; that those professors were all corrupt; that: 'they draw near to me with their lips, but their hearts are far from me, they teach for doctrines the commandments of men, having a form of godliness, but they deny the power thereof'" (Joseph Smith—History 1:15–19).

Joseph could not keep this experience to himself. When he told his family, they received it with reverence. However, when he told some of the ministers in the area about it, his explanation was treated with contempt. They declared that the time of revelation was past and that God would not speak to people today. He was persecuted and ridiculed by these ministers and their supporters.

Three years later, during the night of September 21, 1823, Joseph was praying for a forgiveness of sins and for further help when he had another heavenly manifestation. Suddenly a personage appeared in his room, bathed in brilliant white light, exhibiting radiant purity. This angel announced that he was Moroni, one of God's messengers, and he instructed Joseph about the work God had for him to do, telling him that his name "should be had for good and evil among all nations, kindreds, and tongues, or that it should be both good and evil spoken of among all people" (Joseph Smith—History 1:33).

The angel told him about a book, written upon golden plates, which would give an account of the ancient American people and their origins. Moroni told him that this book contained the fulness of the everlasting gospel and that it would be a new witness for Christ. He told him about two stones in silver bows, fastened to a breastplate, called the Urim and Thummim, which were deposited with the golden plates and could be used to translate them. The angel then stressed several prophecies of great import and departed, the light dissipating and disappearing with him. Two more times that night, the angel appeared and repeated all he had said the first time. The next day, Moroni appeared again, delivering the same message.

The angel led Joseph Smith to a hill in upstate New York called the Hill Cumorah, where he recognized the spot described by the angel and found the buried gold plates and the Urim and Thummim. He was forbidden to remove the contents of the box in which these sacred objects were buried but was challenged to visit this site each year until the plates and the Urim and Thummim were delivered to him for translation. (See Exodus 28:30; Leviticus 8:8; Numbers 27:21; Deuteronomy 33:8; 1 Samuel 28:6; Ezra 2:63; and Nehemiah 7:65.) Only a third of the plates were translated into the Book of Mormon. The angel took back the plates for safekeeping until they would be revealed at a later time, but not before three witnesses had seen the plates and also the angel Moroni. Eight other witnesses saw the plates but not the angel. All of the witnesses testified publicly to what they saw. (Their testimonies are printed in the first few pages of the Book of Mormon.) None ever denied his testimony.

Wasn't this experience of the young Joseph Smith the fulfillment of John the Beloved's prophecy in Revelation 14:6–7?

"I saw another angel fly in the midst of heaven, having the everlasting gospel to preach unto them that dwell on the earth, and to every nation, and kindred, and tongue, and people. Saying with a loud voice, Fear God, and give glory to him; for the hour of his judgment is come: and worship him that made heaven, and earth, and the sea, and the fountains of waters." After all, Moroni told Joseph Smith that the deposited book contained the "fulness of the everlasting gospel" (Joseph Smith—History 1:34).

Having considered the doctrines explained in this book, it is not difficult to believe that Joseph Smith was filled with the Holy Ghost and had the experience of seeing God and Christ standing in the air before him. This was precisely the experience of the first Christian martyr, Stephen, before he was stoned to death: "He, being full of the Holy Ghost, looked up steadfastly into heaven, and saw the glory of God, and Jesus standing on the right hand of God, and said, Behold, I see the heavens opened, and the Son of man standing on the right hand of God" (Acts 7:55–56).

It happened to Stephen. It certainly could have happened to

Joseph Smith. I testify that this experience did happen, both to Stephen in ancient times and to Joseph Smith in the nineteenth century.

This experience is one of the reasons Joseph knew so much about the nature of the Godhead. Since he became a prophet of God who received revelations for this modern age, he was able to explain the gospel of Christ in clear and unmistakable terms. It is difficult to believe that he, with his less than three years of formal schooling, could have accomplished all he did without the extra help only God could have given.

Amos 3:7 says, "Surely the Lord God will do nothing, but he revealeth his secret unto his servants the prophets." Deuteronomy 18:22 notes: "When a prophet speaketh in the name of the Lord, if the thing follow not, nor come to pass, that is the thing which the Lord hath not spoken, but the prophet hath spoken it presumptuously: thou shalt not be afraid of him."

THE PROPHECIES OF JOSEPH SMITH

Here is a small sampling of the things Joseph Smith prophesied:

1. He said that his name "should be had for good and evil among all nations, kindreds, and tongues, and that it should be both good and evil spoken of among all people" (Joseph Smith—History 1:33). At the time of this prophecy, Joseph Smith was not yet eighteen years old. In 1823, he was residing in the backwoods frontier of New York State. He possessed no characteristics that would lead one to believe that he would become famous worldwide.

Today, we cannot go anywhere in the world where enlightened people have not heard of the Mormon prophet Joseph Smith. He is either revered as a prophet of God or ridiculed as an impostor. Thousands of books have been written about him, some favorable and many unfavorable. Countless pamphlets have been written about Joseph Smith. Many are anti-Mormon, critical, and in many cases vitriolic. Surely his name has been "good and evil spoken of among all people."

2. On May 18, 1843, Joseph Smith told Judge Stephen A. Douglas, "Judge, you will aspire to the presidency of the United States; and if ever you turn your hand against me or the Latter-day

Saints, you will feel the weight of the hand of the Almighty upon you; and you will live to see and know that I have testified the truth to you; for the conversation of this day will stick to you through life" (*Teachings of the Prophet Joseph Smith*, comp. Joseph Fielding Smith [Salt Lake City: Deseret Book, 1976], 303).

In 1860, Stephen A. Douglas ran for president of the United States and received the Democratic Party nomination on the 23rd of June. He looked like a sure bet to be elected president. His party had polled one-third again as many popular votes in the preceding election as the two opposing parties combined.

But Judge Douglas, even knowing of their righteousness, raised his voice against Joseph Smith and the Latter-day Saints at a time when he could have helped them. He knew the prophet Joseph Smith. He knew the goodness of members of the Mormon Church. Yet he felt that to defend these Mormons might ruin his political opportunities. Some assumed he was attempting to prove Joseph Smith a false prophet.

Joseph Smith's prophecy was made thirty-three years before this presidential election in 1860. Although he was heavily favored, when the electoral votes were counted, Judge Douglas received but twelve votes. He carried only Missouri, the state where terrible persecutions of the Mormons had occurred. A relatively unknown dark horse won the election and proved to be one of the greatest American presidents, Abraham Lincoln.

Less than twelve months later, Stephen A. Douglas died, partially of a broken heart.

3. On August 6, 1842, Joseph Smith prophesied that "the Saints would continue to suffer much affliction and would be driven to the Rocky Mountains, many would apostatize, others would be put to death by our persecutors or lose their lives in consequence of exposure or disease, and some of you will live to go and assist in making settlements and build cities and see the Saints become a mighty people in the midst of the Rocky Mountains" (*Teachings*, 255).

The Mormon Church now has more than fourteen million members. Its worldwide headquarters is in the midst of the Rocky Mountains in Salt Lake City, Utah.

4. In 1832, some twenty-eight years before it was fulfilled in every detail, Joseph Smith foretold the Civil War. This prophecy is

found in the book of modern revelations called the Doctrine and Covenants, in section 87, verses 1 through 4:

"Verily, thus saith the Lord concerning the wars that will shortly come to pass, beginning at the rebellion of South Carolina, which will eventually terminate in the death and misery of many souls; and the time will come that war will be poured out upon all nations, beginning at this place. For behold, the Southern States shall be divided against the Northern States, and the Southern States will call on other nations, even the nation of Great Britain, as it is called, and they shall also call upon other nations, in order to defend themselves against other nations; and then war shall be poured out upon all nations. And it shall come to pass, after many days, slaves shall rise up against their masters, who shall be marshaled and disciplined for war."

Put yourself in the shoes of Joseph Smith. Try to predict what will happen twenty-eight years from now, let alone next year. It is impossible to do so. Yet Joseph Smith predicted:

• The Civil War.
• The war would begin in South Carolina. On November 10, 1860, South Carolina withdrew its representatives and senators, and the Ordinance of Secession was passed about one week later.
• The war would result in the death of many souls, as it did. The North lost 35,528 with 275,175 wounded, while 258,000 Southerners died with 225,000 wounded.
• War would be poured out on all nations, beginning with the Civil War. We have had two world wars and countless other serious conflicts with some still raging. The number of wars rose from 2,678 in the twelfth century to 13,735 in the first twenty-five years of the twentieth century.
• The Southern States would be divided against the Northern States.
• The Southern States would call upon Great Britain. The Southern States did so, and as a result of Great Britain's intrusions, Great Britain had to pay $15 million in damages after the war.
• The Emancipation Proclamation that would come after the war began: "After many days, slaves shall rise up against their masters, who shall be marshaled and disciplined for war."

Joseph Smith made many other interesting prophecies. The

WHY ARE WE HERE?

Prophet Jeremiah said, "When the word of the prophet shall come to pass, then shall the prophet be known, that the Lord hath truly sent him" (Jeremiah 28:9).

Perhaps more important than Joseph Smith's many prophecies were some of his revelations of knowledge from the Lord:

- The words of angels.
- A translation of a document written by John the Revelator.
- Beautiful prayers.
- Various revelations directed to private individuals.
- Revelations about the priesthood and its history.
- Stupendous visions, including section 76 of the Doctrine and Covenants, which contains an account of five visions dealing with God the Father, his Son Jesus Christ, Satan, and the future glory and destiny of mankind. Section 110 is the description of four visions in which the Savior, Moses, Elias, and Elijah gave instructions or important keys necessary for the work of the restoration.
- Various items of instruction from the Lord.
- God's law of health, the "Word of Wisdom," which, more than a hundred years ago, warned of the dangers of alcohol and tobacco, dangers that have been medically proven today.
- A revelation on eternal marriage.
- Revelations on faith, hope, charity, the nature of God, salvation for the dead, temple work, the latter days, and numerous other spiritual and temporal matters.

Probably the most important tangible evidence of Joseph Smith's prophetic calling is the Book of Mormon itself.

CHAPTER 16

THE BOOK OF MORMON

When ye shall receive these things, I would exhort you that ye would ask God, the Eternal Father, in the name of Christ, if these things are not true; and if ye shall ask with a sincere heart, with real intent, having faith in Christ, he will manifest the truth of it unto you, by the power of the Holy Ghost. And by the power of the Holy Ghost ye may know the truth of all things.

—MORONI 10:4–5

I KNEW A COUPLE who lived in Michigan. Their marriage was on the rocks, and they were headed for the divorce court. Neither was doing the will of the Lord at the time. Each was living an untoward life of sin.

The wife wanted to save the marriage, but she was frustrated and didn't quite know what to do. So one day she decided to take her frustrations and yearnings to the Lord in prayer.

That night, she dreamed she was down in the basement, cleaning out the furnace. She was all covered with soot when a knock came at the door. Two young men in dark apparel were standing there. They told her they had the truth for her.

She never told her husband about this dream, but she could not get it out of her mind.

Sure enough, one day she was down in the basement cleaning out her furnace, all covered with soot, when a knock came at the door. Two young Mormon missionaries were standing there. They told her they had the truth for her and asked if they could come in. She told them she would rather they came back at a more convenient time. Of course, they did.

As they taught this receptive investigator the gospel, she became more and more convinced of the truthfulness of their message. Always her husband refused to discuss anything with the missionaries. Every time she raised the issue, he simply refused to talk about it.

Still, she always left a copy of the Book of Mormon and Church pamphlets in plain view. But he never seemed interested.

Finally, she came to the conclusion that she must be baptized, but she fretted over the confrontation with her husband. He had always snarled when she mentioned the missionaries.

Getting up her courage, she finally decided to talk with her husband about her decision to be baptized. She gingerly approached him. "Dear?" she said.

"What?" he demanded.

She decided to face him head on: "I've decided to be baptized into The Church of Jesus Christ of Latter-day Saints—the Mormons."

"So have I!" he exclaimed.

"What? You haven't even listened to the missionaries."

"Yes, but when I got home that first night, I saw the Book of Mormon lying on the mantel. I picked it up and threw it into the wastebasket. But I had second thoughts. It wasn't my book. And that book is magnetic. As I picked it out of the wastebasket, I couldn't put it down until I had read it. I too have a testimony of its truthfulness, and I too want to be baptized."

No one could have been more pleasantly surprised than the wife. Both were baptized. Their marriage became solid and full of spirituality, humor, uplift, love, and fulfillment. A uniting force—a belief in the truthfulness of the gospel of Jesus Christ—fulfilled both.

PROPHECIES ABOUT THE BOOK OF MORMON

In the Old Testament book of Ezekiel 37:15–17, the prophet seems to be talking about two books: "The word of the Lord came . . . unto me, saying, Moreover, thou son of man, take thee one stick, and write upon it, For Judah, and for the children of Israel his companions: then take another stick, and write upon it, For Joseph, the stick of Ephraim, and for all the house of Israel his companions: and join them one to another into one stick; and they shall become one in thine hand."

The Lord, through the prophet Ezekiel, is clearly prophesying about two sticks or books that shall be joined together in the last days. Since "books" in that day and age were scrolls rolled on sticks, he was clearly talking about a scriptural history of Judah (the biblical history of the Jews) and a scriptural history of the descendants of Joseph, one of Judah's other eleven brothers.

Judah and Joseph's sons, Ephraim and Manasseh, were the progenitors of three of the twelve tribes of Israel. Naturally, they were record-keeping peoples, as taught by the prophets. So, we must not only be looking for the scriptural history of the Jews (the Bible), but also the scriptural history of the tribes of Ephraim and Manasseh, the sons of Joseph. Where is this scriptural history of Joseph or Ephraim and Manasseh? It must be joined together with the scriptural history of the Jews. If these two records are to be joined together, we must obtain both of them.

It is important to know more about Joseph, Judah's brother, whose sons were Ephraim and Manasseh. These two sons took their places as heads of two of the tribes of Israel when one of the twelve sons of Israel was deemed unworthy. In Genesis 49:22–26, Father Jacob, or Israel, gave his patriarchal (father's prophetic) blessing on the head of Joseph, prophesying what was going to happen to Joseph's posterity in the future: "Joseph is a fruitful bough, even a fruitful bough by a well; whose branches run over the wall: The archers have sorely grieved him, and shot at him, and hated him: but his bow abode in strength, and the arms of his hands were made strong by the hands of the mighty God of Jacob; (from thence is the shepherd, the stone of Israel:) even by the God of thy father, who shall help thee; and by the Almighty, who shall bless thee with blessings of heaven above, blessings of the deep that lieth under, blessings of the breasts, and of the womb: the blessings of thy father have prevailed above the blessings of my progenitors unto the utmost bound of the everlasting hills: they shall be on the head of Joseph, and on the crown of the head of him that was separate from his brethren."

This is beautiful allegorical language. Joseph is a "fruitful bough"—a father of a great posterity. He is going to have many descendants. They would be "by a well" or a body of water. His "branches" would "run over the wall"—the ocean. The archers, who hated him, would shoot at him, yet his "bow abode in strength, and the arms of his hands were made strong" by God. He would be blessed with blessings from "heaven above." He and his descendants would have many children—"blessings of the breasts, and of the womb." And, most important, his posterity would inherit the "utmost bound of the everlasting hills."

Who are these descendants of Joseph? Where is the land of the "everlasting hills"? If God has blessed them as this prophecy states, who are they? Where are they? Where is the record pertaining to them?

The "utmost bound of the everlasting hills" seems to refer to the North and South American continents—the only continents in the world with a string of everlasting hills (mountains) from the northern tip of North America to the southern tip of South America.

Remember, in Ezekiel 37:15–17, the record of Joseph is to be joined in the last days with the record of Judah (the Bible). We have the Bible. Where is the record of Joseph? Surely the biblical prophecy must come to pass.

If we could find this scriptural account of the posterity of Joseph's sons Ephraim and Manasseh, it would be an invaluable treasure.

The Bible is the historical and religious account of the ancient Jewish people. God raised up prophets in the holy land and gave them revelations, which they recorded as scripture. Today we know these scriptures as the Bible.

Yet there were other people in the world at the same time.

For instance, there was a great civilization in the Western Hemisphere, the Americas.

Surely, the people there needed God's help as much as the Hebrews.

Surely, God loved them as much as those in the Middle East.

Surely, God is no respecter of persons (Acts 10:34).

Surely, God must have spoken to them through prophets as well.

Surely, we should find a historical and religious record of them.

When the angel Moroni appeared to Joseph Smith on multiple occasions, he told him about a buried record in a hill in upstate New

York, the Hill Cumorah. Ultimately, Joseph Smith was permitted to take the record and, with the help of the Urim and Thummim, translate one-third of it and publish it as the Book of Mormon, the historical and religious account of the ancient American people. The angel Moroni claimed to be the resurrected last prophet of ancient America—the one who had buried the records in the Hill Cumorah in approximately AD 421.

Joseph Smith, an unlearned farm boy, retrieved this record from the ground. With the inspiration and help of God, he translated one-third of the metal plates and published the translation as the Book of Mormon in 1830.

In Revelation 14:6–7, John the Beloved, on the Isle of Patmos, saw "another angel fly in the midst of heaven, having the everlasting gospel to preach unto them that dwell on the earth, and to every nation, and kindred, and tongue, and people, saying with a loud voice, Fear God, and give glory to him; for the hour of his judgment is come: and worship him that made heaven, and earth, and the sea, and the fountains of waters."

When the angel, who introduced himself as Moroni, appeared to Joseph Smith, he said "there was a book deposited, written upon gold plates, giving an account of the former inhabitants of this continent, and the source from whence they sprang. He also said that *the fulness of the everlasting Gospel was contained in it*, as delivered by the Savior to the ancient inhabitants" (Joseph Smith—History 1:34). This was in fulfillment of the prophecy in Revelation 14:6–7.

A FULFILLMENT OF A PROPHECY OF ISAIAH

Isn't the Book of Mormon the record referred to in Isaiah 29:1–4: "Woe to Ariel, to Ariel [Jerusalem], the city where David dwelt! add ye year to year; let them kill sacrifices. Yet I will distress Ariel, and there shall be heaviness and sorrow: and it shall be unto me as Ariel [clearly talking about some other people]. And I will camp against thee round about, and will lay siege against thee with a mount, and I will raise forts against thee. *And thou shalt be brought down, and shall speak out of the ground, and thy speech shalt be low out of the dust,* and thy voice shall be, as of one that hath a familiar spirit, *out of the ground, and thy speech shall whisper out of the dust.*"

Prophetically, these passages of scripture talk about "Ariel," another name for Jerusalem. In the middle of this prophecy about Jerusalem, the prophet shifts to another area that "shall be unto me as Ariel." To what geographical area and people was he referring? He refers to a people who "shalt be brought down, and shalt speak out of the ground . . . low out of the dust."

The Book of Mormon was translated from golden plates found in the ground or dust. It speaks of Jerusalem, or Ariel. Also, it speaks of the ancient American people who wrote upon these plates and preserved them for centuries by burying them in the ground until Joseph Smith was permitted to retrieve them. With the help of God, he translated the plates into the Book of Mormon.

The Book of Mormon literally came from the ground. It speaks out of the dust. It has been referred to as a "voice from the dust."

Joseph was able to translate only one-third of the metal plates because two-thirds were sealed. But, the angel assured him, the last of this record is yet to come forth.

While Joseph Smith was translating the Book of Mormon, Martin Harris, a respected local farmer, got a copy of some of the characters from the plates and took them to a professor Charles Anthon in New York City.

Harris described his experiences as follows: "I went to the city of New York, and presented the characters which had been translated, with the translation thereof, to Professor Charles Anthon, a gentleman celebrated for his literary attainments. Professor Anthon stated that the translation was correct, more so than any he had before seen translated from the Egyptian. I then showed him those which were not yet translated, and he said that they were Egyptian, Chaldaic, Assyriac, and Arabic; and he said they were true characters. He gave me a certificate, certifying to the people of Palmyra that they were true characters, and that the translation of such of them as had been translated was also correct. I took the certificate and put it into my pocket, and was just leaving the house, when Mr. Anthon called me back, and asked me how the young man found out that there were gold plates in the place where he found them. I answered that an angel of God had revealed it unto him.

"He then said to me, 'Let me see that certificate.' I accordingly took it out of my pocket and gave it to him, when he took it and tore it to pieces, saying that there was no such thing now as ministering of angels, and that if I would bring the plates to him he would translate them. I informed him that part of the plates were sealed, and that I was forbidden to bring them. He replied, 'I cannot read a sealed book.' I left him and went to Dr. [Samuel] Mitchell, who sanctioned what Professor Anthon had said respecting both the characters and the translation" (Joseph Smith—History 1:64–65).

In 1834, Professor Charles Anthon vehemently denied he had told Martin Harris the Book of Mormon characters resembled Egyptian characters. However, shortly after Martin Harris's visit with him, in 1831 William W. Phelps wrote a letter in which he stated that Anthon had translated some of the characters. He said they were "the ancient shorthand Egyptian."

Where else could Harris have gotten the phrase "shorthand Egyptian?"

That phrase was a scholarly one that Harris would not have been privy to. In 1824, Champollion had used basically the same term, "tachygraphie," something Anthon would undoubtedly have read, in describing a hieratic Egyptian script. In June 1827, the book in which Champollion was quoted was reviewed in the *American Quarterly Review*, wherein the hieratic Egyptian script was called "short-hand" Egyptian. Anthon had a copy of this and could have read it only months before Harris's visit.

Anthon did deny the story in 1834. He also wrote to anti-Mormon Eber D. Howe, claiming he did not give Harris a written statement. However, in a later letter in 1841 to T. W. Coit, Professor Anthon admitted that he had done so.

Anthon admitted Harris had come to him but left with the "express declaration" that he was *not* going to mortgage his farm or do anything further to help with the printing of the Book of Mormon. Harris must have left fully satisfied, because he did mortgage his farm and totally supported Joseph Smith and the Book of Mormon thereafter.

Then why the discrepancy between Anthon's letter to E. D. Howe and his letter to T. W. Coit? He must have been protecting his standing with his intellectual peers. It would have been professionally difficult for Anthon to have been linked with the Book of Mormon and Joseph Smith, a man constantly and falsely ridiculed in the yellow press for "roguery."

Some forty years later, in 1868, in a "Commemorative Address," Anthon's successor at Columbia College declared that the episode was a real threat to Anthon's reputation.

Most important, this was a fulfillment of the prophecies in Isaiah 29:11–14, wherein Isaiah prophesied: "The vision of all is become unto you as the words of a book *that is sealed*, which men deliver to one that is learned, saying, Read this, I pray thee: and he saith, *I cannot; for it is sealed.* And the book is delivered to him that is not learned, saying, Read this, I pray thee: and he saith, I am not learned. Wherefore the Lord said, Forasmuch as this people draw near me with their mouth, and with their lips do honour me, but have removed their heart far from me, and their fear toward me is taught by the precept of men: therefore, behold, I will proceed to do a marvellous work among this people, even a marvellous work and a wonder: for the wisdom of their wise men shall perish, and the understanding of their prudent men shall be hid."

This experience of Martin Harris was a literal fulfillment of Isaiah's prophecy. Joseph Smith was that unlearned person, and Charles Anthon was the learned one.

Martin Harris was a solid, honest, and dependable citizen. No one can find anything to criticize about his reputation. Anthon admitted to meeting with Harris, but in the attempt to salvage his reputation, he lied and sold his birthright for a mess of intellectual pottage.

THE STORY OF THE BOOK OF MORMON

The Book of Mormon begins in 600 BC with the family of Lehi. Lehi was a prophet in Jerusalem who received revelation about the coming destruction of Jerusalem during the reign of King Zedekiah. Lehi was told to flee and that the Lord would guide him, his family, and a few others to a "promised land."

They wandered in the wilderness for eight years until they were told how to build a ship. Then they were commanded to embark for the promised land and were guided to the Americas.

The family of Lehi eventually divided into two nations: the Nephites, who were lighter-skinned, and the Lamanites, who were darker-skinned progenitors of the Native Americans.

The Book of Mormon is a new witness for Christ and contains

many testimonies of Christ throughout its pages. The Nephites and the Lamanites continually warred against each other. Most often the Nephites were the more righteous but, on occasion, the righteousness of the Lamanites exceeded the Nephites. Prophets in this Western Hemisphere with names like Nephi, Jacob, Enos, Jarom, Omni, Mosiah, Alma, Helaman, Mormon, and Moroni enlighten us with their writings about Christ and his gospel.

Christ, in the meridian of time, made a startling statement in John 10:16, speaking to the Jews: "Other sheep I have, which are not of this fold: them also I must bring, and they shall hear my voice; and there shall be one fold, and one shepherd."

Some thought he must have been referring to the Gentiles, but that is not so. In Matthew 15:24, Christ said, "I am not sent but unto the lost sheep of the house of Israel." So Christ's mission at that time was not to the Gentiles but to the lost sheep of the house of Israel. The Book of Mormon makes it clear in 1 Nephi 6:2 that these early Americans were descendants of Israel. Nephi said, "It sufficeth me to say that we are descendants of Joseph." Joseph was the son of Israel who had the coat of many colors, was sold into Egypt, and became the salvation of Israel.

Then who were these "other sheep" who were "not of this fold" in Jerusalem? Where were they?

The Book of Mormon tells us that Christ, as a resurrected being, came to America. He told those he visited, "Ye are they of whom I said: Other sheep I have which are not of this fold; them also I must bring, and they shall hear my voice; and there shall be one fold, and one shepherd" (3 Nephi 15:21).

Thus we have more words of Christ as ancient American prophets recorded them. These chapters of his visit as a resurrected being are absolutely fascinating and beautiful. He taught his gospel here in the Americas centuries before European settlers arrived to inhabit the New World.

THE BOOK OF MORMON ON BAPTISM

The resurrected Christ taught these people the true nature of Christian baptism. Remember that Paul said there would be one Lord, one faith, one baptism? Christ explained the true nature of baptism and gave the people in this hemisphere the authority to baptize: "The Lord said unto [Nephi]: I give unto you power that ye shall baptize this people when I am again ascended into heaven. And again the Lord called others, and said unto them likewise; and *he gave unto them power to baptize.* And he said unto them: On this wise shall ye baptize; and there shall be no disputations among you. Verily I say unto you, that whoso repenteth of his sins through your words, and desireth to be baptized in my name, on this wise shall ye baptize them—Behold, ye shall go down and stand in the water, and in my name shall ye baptize them. And now behold, these are the words which ye shall say, calling them by name, saying: *Having authority given me of Jesus Christ, I baptize you in the name of the Father, and of the Son, and of the Holy Ghost. Amen. And then shall ye immerse them in the water, and come forth again out of the water"* (3 Nephi 11:21–26).

With those instructions, there is no doubt of the true doctrine of baptism—who should perform it and how it should be performed. The Book of Mormon is explicit on this subject.

But why should we be baptized?

The Book of Mormon gives us the answer: "No unclean thing can enter into his kingdom; therefore nothing entereth into his rest save it be those who have washed their garments in my blood, because of their faith, and the repentance of all their sins, and their faithfulness unto the end. Now this is the commandment: Repent, all ye ends of the earth, and come unto me and be baptized in my name, *that ye may be sanctified by the reception of the Holy Ghost, that ye may stand spotless before me at the last day"* (3 Nephi 27:19–20).

THE BEATITUDES IN THE BOOK OF MORMON

Christ gave his Sermon on the Mount to the Nephites but with some notable differences from his sermon in Palestine. We will examine only a few of the verses to give their flavor. It may be helpful to compare some of the scriptures as recorded in the King James Version of the Bible to the beatitudes recorded in the Book of Mormon:

The Bible: "Blessed are the poor in spirit: for theirs is the kingdom of heaven" (Matthew 5:3). What is meant by the "poor in spirit?" The drunk down on the corner is "poor in spirit." So is the person on death row. Is theirs the kingdom of heaven? No.

The Book of Mormon: "Yea, blessed are the poor in spirit *who come unto me*, for theirs is the kingdom of heaven" (3 Nephi 12:3). The additional four words, "who come unto me," clarify this beatitude and fulfill its meaning.

The Bible: "Blessed are they which do hunger and thirst after righteousness: for they shall be filled" (Matthew 5:6). What are they to be filled with? Is it love, faith, honor, virtue, happiness, kindness?

The Book of Mormon: "And blessed are all they who do hunger and thirst after righteousness, for they shall be filled with the Holy Ghost" (3 Nephi 12:6). What greater gift could those who search after righteousness obtain than the gift of the Holy Ghost? How much more clear this beatitude becomes in the Book of Mormon!

As you can see, there are noticeable differences in the two versions. The Book of Mormon version is more complete and makes more sense.

THE NAME OF CHRIST'S CHURCH

What should the name of Christ's church be? We have many different churches with many different names. The Book of Mormon is explicit on this subject. In 3 Nephi 27:8 Christ said, "How be it my church save it be called in my name? For if a church be called in Moses' name then it be Moses' church; or if it be called in the name of a man then it be the church of a man; but if it be called in my name then it is my church, *if it so be that they are built upon my gospel.*"

When we review the churches of the world, very few are called by the name of Christ. Offhand it is difficult to name more than a dozen. Certainly, the church should bear the name of Christ. Yet there is one more qualification. The true church of Jesus Christ *must be built upon his gospel.* Therefore, we should look for the name of Christ and then compare the teachings of that church with the true gospel of Jesus Christ as outlined in the scriptures.

That is one of the reasons for this book. It is apparent from the scriptures that The Church of Jesus Christ of Latter-day Saints not only bears the name of Christ but also has the true doctrinal understanding of Christ's gospel.

WE MAY KNOW FOR OURSELVES

One of the greatest teachings of the Book of Mormon is that we can find out for ourselves whether it is true and whether Joseph Smith is a true prophet of God.

In the last chapter of the Book of Mormon, in Moroni 10:4–5, a wonderful promise is given to all who sincerely read and pray about the Book of Mormon: "*When ye shall receive these things, I would exhort you that ye would ask God, the Eternal Father, in the name of Christ, if these things are not true; and if ye shall ask with a sincere heart, with real intent, having faith in Christ, he will manifest the truth of it unto you, by the power of the Holy Ghost. And by the power of the Holy Ghost ye may know the truth of all things.*"

What a powerful promise! Prayerfully turning to God, millions have found the truth that there are prophets in the world today— yes, in our day and age. The advantage of this promise is that we do not have to take anyone's word or follow anyone's teachings other than those of Christ. We can find out for ourselves if the Book of Mormon is true by putting this great promise to the test. Once we do, we will want to embrace the gospel, follow the living prophets, and do all within our power to live the principles of truth.

CONVERTED THROUGH THE BOOK OF MORMON

One of the most interesting testimonies of the Book of Mormon arises out of the conversion of a good friend of mine who died several years ago. Father John Staley had been a Benedictine monk for twenty-five years when he finally met a wonderful woman who helped bring him the Book of Mormon and the gospel. He was the second of sixteen children. His father and uncle had been orphans who were lovingly raised by Benedictine monks of St. Vincent Arch Abbey in Latrobe, Pennsylvania. In fact, John's uncle was the head or abbot of that monastic community. The abbot uncle was John's hero.

At age twelve, John left his family circle and entered St. Vincent's for its prep school, liberal arts college, and seminary training for Catholic priests. After two years of college, he took his first triennial vows as a Benedictine monk. At the age of twenty-five, in 1941, he became a Catholic priest and a devoted servant to the Catholic people.

In 1967, at the age of fifty, he left the community at St. Vincent's. He met Mariellen, his future wife, who brought the young Mormon missionaries to him. He began to see scriptural matters more intensively than at any time in his life. He did not want to leave the Catholic Church and, in fact, was devoted to his fellow monks and priests right up until the time he died.

He obtained a copy of the Book of Mormon and was challenged to put its promise to the test. This he did. Through the Spirit, he obtained a tremendous testimony of the gospel. He was baptized. He married Mariellen and became a sociology professor at Brigham Young University in Provo, Utah.

John never lost his love for the Catholic Church, its priests, monks, and other officials. He visited them, loved them, and cared for them. But he had found the true gospel of Jesus Christ.

Before he died, I asked him to be on my advisory committee for persons with disabilities. He, along with other professionals on that advisory committee, played a significant role in advising me as we wrote the Americans with Disabilities Act—the comprehensive bill guaranteeing civil rights to persons with disabilities.

I know John felt this experience was one of the greatest of his life. I will forever be grateful for his contributions to that effort.

John Staley was one of the greatest men I have known. Once he received the testimony of the Spirit, he did not hesitate to join The Church of Jesus Christ of Latter-day Saints.

Joseph Smith said, "I told the brethren that the Book of Mormon was the most correct of any book on earth, and the keystone to our religion, and a man could get closer to God by abiding by its precepts, than by any other book" (*Teachings*, 194).

Why not put the book's promise to the test by reading it with a prayerful heart, in faith? Find out for yourself if it is true. Ask God if he has placed modern prophets on the earth to help us with our modern problems.

I bear witness that the Book of Mormon is true. The first time I knew it was true was when I was seventeen years old. I read it, prayed about it, and had a profound spiritual experience that impressed upon my mind that it is true and that Joseph Smith was a true prophet of God. That is one reason I am so confident that you too will receive this God-given testimony of the truthfulness of these scriptures if you will read the Book of Mormon and ask with a sincere heart, with real intent, having faith in Christ, if it is not true. I know that God will manifest the truth of it to you by the power of the Holy Ghost.

PART 3

WHERE ARE
WE GOING?

CHAPTER 17

OUR LIFE
AFTER DEATH

The spirits of all men, as soon as they are departed from this mortal body, . . . are taken home to that God who gave them life.

—ALMA 40:11

YOU HAVE PROBABLY had occasion during your life to mourn the death of a loved one. Possibly you have wondered what has become of that person. Possibly you have wondered what will become of you after you die. When we die, the spirit leaves the body. That is what death is—the separation of the body and the spirit. James 2:26 says "the body without the spirit is dead." Where does the spirit go?

THE SPIRIT WORLD

In Luke 16:19–26, the Master's parable explains that the spirit goes to the spirit world: "There was a certain rich man, which was clothed in purple and fine linen, and fared sumptuously every day: and there was a certain beggar named Lazarus, which was laid at his gate, full of sores, and desiring to be fed with the crumbs which fell from the rich man's table: moreover the dogs came and licked his sores. And it came to pass, that the beggar died, and was carried by the angels into Abraham's bosom: the rich man also died, and was buried; and in hell he lift up his eyes, being in torments, and seeth Abraham afar off, and Lazarus in his bosom. And he cried and said, Father Abraham, have mercy on me, and send Lazarus, that he may dip the tip of his finger in water, and cool my tongue; for I am tormented in this flame. But Abraham said, Son, remember that thou in thy lifetime receivedst thy good things, and likewise Lazarus evil things: but now he is comforted, and thou art tormented. And beside all this, between us and you there is a great gulf fixed: so that they which would pass from hence to you cannot; neither can they pass to us, that would come from thence."

We can see from the Lord's parable that the rich man had everything in this life, while Lazarus, the beggar, had nothing but the crumbs from the rich man's table. Yet when the rich man died, he went to a place of torment, which we call hell. Lazarus, who apparently had lived a decent life, went to Abraham's bosom, or a state of paradise. Both men went to a part of the spirit world.

In whose shoes would you like to be: those of Lazarus or those of the rich man? Naturally, Lazarus is the one to emulate. Yet it all depends on what we do while here on the earth.

Lazarus went to a place of comfort, a place of peace called Abraham's bosom. The rich man went to a place of torment. He could see Lazarus on Abraham's bosom but, because of a great gulf, could not receive any comfort from Lazarus to cool his tongue.

This makes it abundantly clear how important our earth life is. It is only a short time in the eternal scheme of things. But our lives here will determine whether we go to Abraham's bosom (a state of paradise) or a place of torment, or hell.

Which will you choose?

Whichever, immediately after death, it is the spirit world we will enter. What happens to us after that?

THE RESURRECTION

Note 1 Corinthians 15:20–22, which explains the next step: "Now is Christ risen from the dead, and become the firstfruits of them that slept. For since by man came death, by man came also the resurrection of the dead. For as in Adam all die, even so in Christ shall all be made alive." In other words, everyone who comes to the earth will be resurrected with a perfect body of flesh and bones to house his or her spirit. That is one of the reasons we shouted for joy at the opportunity of coming here.

In Philippians 3:20–21, Paul explains the resurrected state: "Our conversation is in heaven; from whence also we look for the Saviour, the Lord Jesus Christ: who shall change our vile body, that it may be fashioned like unto his glorious body, according to the working whereby he is able even to subdue all things unto himself." Our resurrected bodies will become like Christ's, to the extent that we will be able to "subdue all things" unto ourselves. We, like the resurrected Christ, will then have power over the elements.

Even so, as great as the resurrection is, John 5:25–29 says, "The hour is coming, and now is, when the dead shall hear the voice of the Son of God: and they that hear shall live. For as the Father hath life in himself; so hath he given to the Son to have life in himself; and hath given him authority to execute judgment also, because he is the Son of man. Marvel not at this: *for the hour is coming, in the which all that are in the graves shall hear his voice, and shall come forth; they that have done good, unto the resurrection of life; and they that have done evil, unto the resurrection of damnation.*"

The scriptures are evidence there will be a resurrection of the just and the unjust. Which do you want to be? It all depends on how you live. This earth life is extremely important! Living the gospel of Christ here will bring joy, peace, comfort, and assurance of blessings, not only in this life but also in the life hereafter with Christ and God.

THE JUDGMENT

After the resurrection, then what? Consider Revelation 20:12: "I saw the dead, small and great, stand before God; and the books were opened: and another book was opened, which is the book of life: and the dead were judged out of those things which were written in the books, according to their works."

So the Day of Judgment will come to each of us. We will be judged in accordance with what we have done here on the earth. This earth life is extremely important.

Again, whose shoes would you like to be in—the rich man's or those of Lazarus? The rich man had an even better chance here on the earth but failed the test because he did not keep God's commandments. Lazarus passed the test and reaped the benefits of being judged a wise and decent man.

Where do we go after the Day of Judgment? Most Christian churches teach that we will go to one of two places—either heaven or hell. And the Catholic Church has the additional concept of purgatory.

What if two people, you and I, are borderline cases? We are not righteous enough to live with the great prophets, priests, and other righteous people. But neither are we so evil that we deserve to go to hell with liars, murderers, whoremongers, and adulterers.

What if I live just slightly better than you and slip into heaven, barely making it in with the prophets, saints, and holiest of people? You barely miss going into heaven because you did one less good deed than I. So you slide into association with the corrupt. Would that be just? Yet there would have to be a great number of borderline cases like this if there are only a heaven and a hell in the life hereafter. How can we justify saying that I go to heaven while you, not really a bad person, go to hell with the dregs of humanity—liars, murderers, and whoremongers? It wouldn't be right. Would a just God do that to you and me?

Surely there must be a better way. Consider what the Savior said in John 14:2: "In my Father's house are *many mansions*: if it were not so, I would have told you. I go to prepare a place for you." Christ talked about many places we might go in the life hereafter.

In Matthew 10:41, a profound scripture, Christ says, "He that receiveth a prophet in the name of a prophet *shall receive a prophet's reward*; and he that receiveth a righteous man in the name of a righteous man *shall receive a righteous man's reward*."

This scripture clearly foretells at least three rewards we may receive when we die: (1) *a prophet's reward*, for those who followed the prophets; (2) *a righteous man's reward*, for those who did not follow the prophets but were nevertheless righteous; (3) the reward (by implication) of the unrighteous, who certainly will *not* go where the righteous or those who followed the prophets will go. Therefore, we can deduce there are at least three places we can go in the life hereafter.

This deduction is confirmed in 1 Corinthians 15:40–43, which says, "There are . . . *celestial bodies*, and *bodies terrestrial*: but the glory of the celestial is one, and the glory of the terrestrial is another. There is one *glory of the sun*, and another *glory of the moon*, and another *glory of the stars*: for one star differeth from another star in glory. *So also is the resurrection of the dead.* It is sown in corruption; it is raised in incorruption."

There will be three degrees of glory where we, as resurrected beings, may go, depending upon our worthiness. These three degrees of glory are compared with the sun, the moon, and the stars. Also, there will be different degrees of glory within each of these degrees of glory (for one star differs from another in glory).

The celestial kingdom is metaphorically compared to the glory of the sun. This is the highest kingdom and the one where God dwells. The terrestrial kingdom is the one where those who reject the prophets but still live good lives will go. The lower kingdom, as designated in latter-day revelation, is the telestial kingdom. That is where the wicked will go. Latter-day revelation tells us that even though the telestial kingdom is where the unrighteous go, its glory is beyond our earthly comprehension.

There must be one other kingdom—that of the devil, Lucifer, the adversary. It is called outer darkness or the kingdom of perdition. That is where the third of the hosts of heaven who were cast out with Lucifer will go, as well as resurrected mortals who are "filthy still," who have murdered by shedding innocent blood after receiving the new and everlasting covenant or who have committed blasphemy against the Holy Ghost (Matthew 12:31; see also John 17:12; 2 Thessalonians 2:3; Hebrews 10:9; 2 Peter 3:7; Revelation 17:8).

Where would Lazarus finally have gone? If he had followed the prophets and lived the gospel on earth, he would have entered the celestial kingdom. How about the rich man? Most likely, he went to the telestial kingdom, which was compared to the stars in the sky. Which do you want to inherit—the celestial, terrestrial, or telestial kingdom? Accepting the prophets and their teachings is the key to inheriting the celestial kingdom of God. To go there, we must humble ourselves and live the gospel taught by Christ and his holy prophets.

CHAPTER 18

SALVATION FOR THE DEAD

It was, thanks no doubt to heavenly power and aid, that the doctrine of salvation like the rays of the sun, suddenly lighted up the whole world.

—EUSEBIUS

ONE OF THE MOST perplexing questions for most Christians is, what happens to all who have never heard of the Bible, Christ, even God, the priesthood, baptism, or any of the gospel? Or, what happens to those who have heard but not accepted the gospel for some reason? What happens to those who believe they have accepted the gospel but, in fact, have belonged to a church that does not have the priesthood? What happens to all who have lived with little or no opportunity to hear the gospel and who have not had the same opportunity for salvation that we have?

Some churches teach that many of these people may be lost or damned. Some churches have no answers to these questions. Some teach that unless all people accept their particular brand of religion, they are damned or lost. Some merely throw up their hands in frustration because they do not know how to answer these questions.

The larger question is, does it seem logical that God, being just, would damn these people without giving each of them an equal opportunity to accept his teachings? No!

Then what happens to the vast majority of the world's prior and present population—that is, non-Christian and those who are unknowledgeable about the gospel of Jesus Christ?

God is just. Then isn't it logical that all people will have the opportunity to hear and either accept or reject the gospel of Christ? If God is no respecter of persons, as stated in Acts 10:34–35, then we must all be given the privilege of accepting or rejecting his gospel. If that is so, then how do we reconcile the fact that billions who have lived on earth have never heard of the gospel, Jesus Christ, the priesthood, or other principles of salvation? Are they irreparably condemned without even a chance? No other religion has an answer to this problem.

"THEY THAT HEAR SHALL LIVE"

Through revelation, we learn some simple eternal truths about this subject of salvation for all. Speaking about the unfortunate people who have not had the opportunity of accepting Christ's gospel, the Prophet Isaiah wrote, "They shall be gathered together, as prisoners are gathered in the pit, and shall be shut up in the prison, and after many days shall they be visited" (Isaiah 24:22).

Naturally, questions arise: What does Isaiah mean by "pit" or "prison"? Who will visit those who dwell there?

In John 5:25–29 we find a partial answer. Speaking of the dead and of the resurrection, Christ explained: "The hour is coming, and now is, when the dead shall hear the voice of the Son of God: and *they that hear shall live.* For as the Father hath life in himself; so hath he given to the Son to have life in himself; and hath given him authority to execute judgment also, because he is the Son of man. Marvel not at this: for the hour is coming, in the which *all that are in the graves shall hear his voice, and shall come forth; they that have done good, unto the resurrection of life; and they that have done evil, unto the resurrection of damnation.*"

Christ will visit the dead, who will hear his voice. Those who listen to him and change their lives "shall live." Christ will have the authority to "execute judgment," and "all that are in the graves shall hear his voice."

Now we see why Isaiah said these people would be "gathered in the pit" and be "shut up in prison," but after many days "they [would] be visited." We now know that Christ is their visitor. Christ's mission is always to teach his gospel. Therefore, if the spirits of the dead hear Christ's voice, as he visits them in the pit or prison, they will hear the gospel of Jesus Christ.

When Christ was on the cross, two thieves or "malefactors" flanked him on both sides (Luke 23:32). "And one of the malefactors which were hanged railed on him, saying, If thou be Christ, save thyself and us." The other malefactor rebuked the first and said, "Dost not thou fear God, seeing thou art in the same condemnation? And we indeed justly; for we receive the due reward of our deeds: but this man hath done nothing amiss. And he said unto Jesus, *Lord, remember me when thou comest into thy kingdom.*" Christ responded, "Verily I say unto thee, *To day* shalt thou be with me in paradise" (Luke 23:39–43).

Where did Christ and the thief go? Paradise.

When? That very day.

Some theologians assert that paradise is simply another word for heaven. That is not so. In John 20:17, after Christ had been resurrected, Mary went to embrace him. Christ said to her, "Touch me not; *for I am not yet ascended to my Father*: but go to my brethren, and say unto them, I ascend unto my Father, and your Father; and to my God, and your God."

Christ and the thief went to paradise that very day. Yet three days later, Christ was resurrected; Mary tried to embrace him, and he said, "Touch me not for I have not yet ascended to my Father," who dwells in heaven. Christ had gone to paradise but had not yet ascended to heaven. Therefore, paradise must be a state of existence between earth life and heaven.

Paradise is part of the spirit world where the righteous go immediately following death. Remember the other part of the spirit world? Yes, it was torment or prison. Could anyone go from one to the other at that time, before Christ's resurrection? No. Why? Because there was "a great gulf fixed: so that they which would pass from hence to you cannot; neither can they pass to us, that would come from thence" (Luke 16:26).

Since Christ went to the Spirit World, he must have had some special reason to do so. Christ does not do unnecessary things. In 1 Peter 3:18–20, his mission is explained: "Christ . . . hath once suffered for sins, the just for the unjust, that he might bring us to God, being put to death in the flesh, but quickened by the Spirit: by which also *he went and preached unto the spirits in prison*; which sometime were disobedient, when once the longsuffering of God waited in the days of Noah, while the ark was a preparing, wherein few, that is, eight souls were saved by water." Peter tells us that Christ's mission was to preach to the spirits in prison. What did Christ preach? He must have preached his gospel.

Remember what separated paradise or Abraham's bosom from the prison? It was the "great gulf." The people could not go from one side of the gulf to the other until Christ bridged the gulf and allowed the gospel to be preached to those in prison. So, one of Christ's missions was to bridge the gulf and make it possible for others, after his visit, to preach the gospel to those in the spirit prison.

In 1 Peter 4:6, we learn why Christ preached the gospel to them in prison: "For this cause *was the gospel preached also to them that are dead, that they might be judged according to men in the flesh, but live according to God in the spirit*." It is easy to deduce that the people who have departed this life will have the opportunity to accept the gospel in the spirit world so they can be judged in the end like those who have the privilege of receiving it here on the earth. More important, if they accept the gospel, they might "live according to God in the spirit," that is, with God in the life hereafter.

Would Christ have wasted his time preaching the gospel to them if there was no opportunity for them to receive it and accept it? No!

BAPTISM FOR THE DEAD

To accept the gospel here on earth, we must obey the first principles and ordinances of the gospel. First, we must have an active belief—faith. Can a spirit have faith? Certainly. Then we must repent. Can a spirit repent of his or her sins? Certainly. But then we must accept the gospel and be baptized, for "Except a man be born of water and of the Spirit, he cannot enter into the kingdom of God" (John 3:5). Of course, baptism is an earthly ordinance, performed with earthly materials. Therefore, can a spirit be baptized? No. So what happens? Here we have spirits who have accepted the gospel, had faith, and repented but now cannot be baptized because they are no longer in the flesh.

Think about it. Would Christ have preached the gospel to them if no way was provided for them to be baptized and gain their salvation? No! Yet, they cannot be baptized for themselves. What can be done?

Consider 1 Corinthians 15:29: "What shall they do which *are baptized for the dead*, if the dead rise not at all? why are they then baptized for the dead?" Here, Paul explains that the early Christians were "baptizing for the dead." He didn't say baptism of the dead but baptism for the dead. This verse makes it clear that someone on earth must be baptized vicariously for each of those who have passed on but who have accepted the gospel in the spirit world.

This vicarious act isn't odd. After all, who performed the greatest vicarious act in history? Christ died that, through him, all of us might gain salvation. Christ's greatest work was to bring about the opportunity of salvation for all mankind.

We have been directed through latter-day revelation to search out the genealogies of our ancestors. Then we must send the information to the temples of the Church, where this special ordinance of vicarious baptism for those who have passed on is performed. Thus, a greater work will have been performed for billions of people who, having had the gospel presented to them in the spirit world, may accept the gospel and receive all of the benefits thereof.

In John 14:12, Christ said, "He that believeth on me, the works that I do shall he do also; and greater works than these shall he do; because I go unto my Father." Christ's greatest work was to give us salvation, yet he tells us in John that we will do the same work. By seeking out the genealogy of those who have passed on and by vicariously going to the temple and being baptized for them, we are providing a means for those in the spirit world to gain their salvation.

It is a wonderful concept that all people will have the opportunity sometime in their journey through eternity—either here on earth or in the spirit world—to gain salvation.

This vicarious work is part of the work performed in the beautiful temples of The Church of Jesus Christ of Latter-day Saints. We are expected to do this work because God has "provided some better thing for us, that they without us should not be made perfect" (Hebrews 11:40).

In Malachi 4:5–6 we read one of the greatest prophecies concerning the last days: "I will send you Elijah the prophet before the coming of the great and dreadful day of the Lord: and he shall turn the heart of the fathers to the children, and the heart of the children to their fathers, lest I come and smite the earth with a curse."

Malachi prophesied that before Christ came the second time, Elijah the prophet must come. On April 3, 1836, Joseph Smith and Oliver Cowdery were visited by Elijah the prophet, "who was taken to heaven without tasting death" (Doctrine and Covenants 110:13). Elijah stood before them and said, "Behold, the time has fully come, which was spoken of by the mouth of Malachi—testifying that [I] should be sent, before the great and dreadful day of the Lord come— To turn the hearts of the fathers to the children, and the children to the fathers, lest the whole earth be smitten with a curse—Therefore, the keys of this dispensation are committed into your hands; and by this ye may know that the great and dreadful day of the Lord is near, even at the doors" (Doctrine and Covenants 110:14–16).

Through the work in the temples, including the gathering of genealogical information, the hearts of the children are turned to their fathers. Those waiting for the work to be done are the fathers whose hearts are turned to their children.

CHAPTER 19

ETERNAL MARRIAGE

Adam could not be happy even in Paradise without Eve.

—John Lubbock

HAVE YOU EVER WONDERED what will happen to your family in the hereafter? What will happen to your parents and your brothers and sisters? What will happen to your spouse and children? The family is the most important reason for living and enjoying this earthly life. Will it be dissolved once we die? Or will we be together in the hereafter? Is there a way we can be married for more than "till death do us part"?

One of the reasons for Mormon temples is the performance of sealings, or eternal marriages, for loving couples who dedicate themselves and their families to being worthy to be together forever.

The Savior, speaking to Peter in Matthew 16:19, said, "I will give unto thee the keys of the kingdom of heaven: and whatsoever thou shalt bind on earth shall be bound in heaven: and whatsoever thou shalt loose on earth shall be loosed in heaven."

That power to bind is further described in Mark 10:7–9: "A man [shall] leave his father and mother, and cleave to his wife; and they twain shall be one flesh: so then they are no more twain, but one flesh. *What therefore God hath joined together, let not man put asunder.*"

This is further illustrated in 1 Corinthians 11:11: "Neither is the man without the woman, neither the woman without the man, in the Lord."

The Lord's plan is to elevate families to the highest place of significance in our lives. To do so, he provides a way for families to be eternal. If men and women, as equal and spiritual partners, rear children righteously while showing respect and kindness for each other, they can be bound together by one having authority to perform eternal marriages. Families can be united eternally in the presence of God. That gives new meaning to the importance of marriage, family, children, and our lives together.

Paul gave this counsel to husbands: "Love your wives, even as Christ also loved the church, and gave himself for it" (Ephesians 5:25). In Ephesians 5:28 he wrote: "So ought men to love their wives as their own bodies. He that loveth his wife loveth himself." Additionally, in Ephesians 5:33 we read, "Let every one of you in particular so love his wife even as himself; and the wife see that she reverence her husband."

In the compilation of modern revelations called the Doctrine and Covenants, Joseph Smith wrote: "In the celestial glory there are three heavens or degrees; and in order to obtain the highest, a man must enter into this order of the priesthood [meaning the new and everlasting covenant of marriage]; and if he does not, he cannot obtain it. He may enter into the other, but that is the end of his kingdom; he cannot have an increase" (D&C 131:1–4).

In the 132nd section of the Doctrine and Covenants, verses 15–16, the Lord said, "If a man marry him a wife in the world, and he marry her not by me nor by my word, and he covenant with her so long as he is in the world and she with him, their covenant and marriage are not of force when they are dead, and when they are out of the world; therefore, they are not bound by any law when they are out of the world. Therefore, when they are out of the world they neither marry nor are given in marriage; but are appointed angels in heaven, which angels are ministering servants, to minister for those who are worthy of a far more, and an exceeding, and an eternal weight of glory."

In Doctrine and Covenants section 132:19, the Lord expanded that statement: "If a man marry a wife by my word, which is my law, and by the new and everlasting covenant, and it is sealed unto them by the Holy Spirit of promise, by him who is anointed, unto whom I have appointed this power and the keys of this priesthood; . . . it shall be said unto them—Ye shall come forth in the first resurrection; and if it be after the first resurrection, in the next resurrection; and shall inherit thrones, kingdoms, principalities, and powers, dominions, all heights and depths."

One of the latter-day apostles, Bruce R. McConkie, summed it up this way: "The most important things that any member of The Church of Jesus Christ of Latter-day Saints ever does in this world are: 1) To marry the right person, in the right place, by the right authority; and 2) To keep the covenant made in connection with this holy and perfect order of matrimony, thus assuring the obedient persons of an inheritance of exaltation in the celestial kingdom" (*Mormon Doctrine*, 2nd ed. [Salt Lake City: Bookcraft, 1966], 118).

CHAPTER 20

A FINAL
TESTIMONY

I HAVE WRITTEN this book because of the need for a short primer explaining the beautiful doctrines of The Church of Jesus Christ of Latter-day Saints. It is intended for those investigating the Church, the missionaries who teach them, new converts to the Church, those who are young and learning, and those who are interested in studying the doctrines of the Church.

One of the great blessings of my life is having seen many people search the scriptures, read the Book of Mormon, listen to the missionaries, and join the Church. I have seen Catholic priests, ministers of other faiths, Jewish people, agnostics, atheists, and many others read the Book of Mormon, gain a testimony of the gospel, and join the Church.

When I reached the age of seventeen, having had faith in my religion throughout my youth, I decided to find out for myself if the Book of Mormon was true. I took the challenge of the Book of Mormon to read it and to pray about it with real intent and with faith in Jesus Christ. I can still recall being in my humble, unheated, and sparsely furnished upstairs bedroom when I finished reading the book. I was overcome by the Spirit witnessing to me that the Book of Mormon is true. Ever since that eventful evening, I have been able to bear testimony of its truthfulness.

When I was twelve years old, my parents took me to an old farmer-patriarch in the little town of Smithfield, Utah, who did not know my parents or me, for a patriarchal blessing. (Remember

Jacob's patriarchal blessing on his son Joseph, mentioned earlier in this book.) I was the son of a skilled laborer and knew nothing about government, the Constitution, or any other political matters. As a young boy, my only goals were to become a builder like my father (which I later came to be) and to become a good athlete. I had no other ideas about the future. The prophetic blessing the old patriarch gave me was simple yet profound.

Patriarchal blessings are extremely personal, so I will not share much of it, but you will be interested in just two sentences in the middle of the blessing: "Thou shalt be privileged to mingle with people of many types of character and learning, and shalt have contacts with men and women of educational attainments, and holding high and responsible positions of leadership among the people. These contacts will help thee to ripen in wisdom and judgment." Surely these promises have come to pass. But these two sentences are by no means the most important sentences in my blessing. The blessing prophesies many other astounding things, and I cannot read it without amazement at the inspiration of that old farmer-patriarch sixty-six years ago. He predicted a great number of things that have already come to pass and some that are still to occur.

About the time I received my patriarchal blessing, which promised me that my life would be spared, a friend and I were going home from a Sunday double-header baseball game when I got off the bus and ran across the road. Unfortunately, I didn't see the automobile that was coming down the road at fifty miles per hour. It hit me head-on and threw me sixty feet, twelve feet in the air. At that moment, my father and a friend were coming around the corner and saw it all. I was picked up unconscious, with a serious concussion and other unknown internal injuries, and taken to the hospital. The elders of the Church administered to me (blessed me), and I awoke with only a bruised hip and a headache. My life was miraculously spared. I also learned an important lesson from this experience— keep the Sabbath day holy.

I have personally had the experience of exercising the Melchizedek Priesthood, which was conferred upon me. I have seen the power of the priesthood, as stated in James 5:14–15: "Is any sick among you? let him call for the elders of the church; and let them pray over him, anointing him with oil in the name of the

Lord: and the prayer of faith shall save the sick, and the Lord shall raise him up; and if he have committed sins, they shall be forgiven him."

I have had the privilege of representing the Lord and administering these blessings to numerous people. I have seen the lame walk, the blind see, the barren have children, and the chronically ill be healed. I have seen people receive the gift of faith. I have seen chronic nausea dispelled, lives saved, and people healed in a wide variety of ways. These have been wonderful spiritual experiences to me.

I have personally known a number of the modern prophets, from David O. McKay to the present prophet, Thomas S. Monson. I have felt and recognized their inspiration as apostles and prophets. I know that the Lord raised each of them up for specific purposes. How blessed we are to have prophets in this day to guide us and help us with the myriad problems of our complex modern society.

The gospel of Jesus Christ is true. I know that beyond any doubt and have expressed my testimony on many occasions to friendly and not-so-friendly audiences. That knowledge transcends any other knowledge I have obtained in life. Nothing else is as important as knowing that Jesus Christ atoned for our sins, died, was resurrected, and paved the way for us to return to our Father in Heaven with our families.

It is my hope and prayer that this little book will be of interest to you and your family as evidence of the truthfulness of the beautiful gospel of Jesus Christ. I express my love and my thanks that you have taken time to read it. God bless you.

THE ARTICLES OF FAITH

OF THE CHURCH OF JESUS CHRIST
OF LATTER-DAY SAINTS

1   We believe in God, the Eternal Father, and in His Son, Jesus
    Christ, and in the Holy Ghost.

2   We believe that men will be punished for their own sins, and
    not for Adam's transgression.

3   We believe that through the Atonement of Christ, all man-
    kind may be saved, by obedience to the laws and ordinances
of the Gospel.

4   We believe that the first principles and ordinances of the Gospel
    are: first, Faith in the lord Jesus Christ; second, Repentance;
third, Baptism by immersion for the remission of sins; fourth, laying
on of hands for the gift of the Holy Ghost.

5   We believe that a man must be called of God, by prophecy,
    and by the laying on of hands by those who are in authority, to
preach the Gospel and administer in the ordinances thereof.

6 We believe in the same organization that existed in the Primitive Church, namely, apostles, prophets, pastors, teachers, evangelists, and so forth.

7 We believe in the gift of tongues, prophecy, revelation, visions, healing, interpretation of tongues, and so forth.

8 We believe the Bible to be the word of God as far as it is translated correctly; we also believe the Book of Mormon to be the word of God.

9 We believe all that God has revealed, all that He does now reveal, and we believe that He will yet reveal many great and important things pertaining to the Kingdom of God.

10 We believe in the literal gathering of Israel and in the restoration of the Ten Tribes; that Zion (the New Jerusalem) will be built upon the American continent; that Christ will reign personally upon the earth; and, that the earth will be renewed and receive its paradisiacal glory.

11 We claim the privilege of worshiping Almighty God according to the dictates of our own conscience, and allow all men the same privilege, let them worship how, where, or what they may.

12 We believe in being subject to kings, presidents, rulers, and magistrates, in obeying, honoring, and sustaining the law.

13 We believe in being honest, true, chaste, benevolent, virtuous, and in doing good to all men; indeed, we may say that we follow the admonition of Paul—We believe all things, we hope all things, we have endured many things, and hope to be able to endure all things. If there is anything virtuous, lovely, or of good report or praiseworthy, we seek after these things.

SCRIPTURE INDEX

SUBJECT
INDEX

A

Abortion, woman who
repented of, 35–37
Abraham and the sacrifice of
Isaac, 28–29
Adam, 10, 25–27
Adultery, 47–48
Agency, 39, 40–41
Anthon, Charles, and Book of
Mormon translation, 110–12
Apostasy, 87–93
Apostles, 76–78; in modern
day, 88
Articles of Faith, 56
Athanasian creed, 7–8
Atonement of Jesus Christ,
27–34, 63: was voluntary,
27; as sign of God's love,
29; Jesus Christ qualified
to make, 31; in modern
revelation, 31–34; necessity
of, 32–33; made repentance
possible, 63
Authority. *See* Priesthood

B

Baptism: as outward sign of
faith, 65–66; correct form
of, 65–68; necessity of, 66;
Greek origin of word, 67;
authority to perform, 65, 68,
71–72, 83–84; of infants
and children, 68–70; in the
Book of Mormon, 113–14;
of the dead, 130–32
Bearing false witness, 49
Beatitudes in the Book of
Mormon, 114–15
Bible Commentary, 44
Body: Satan and followers do
not have, 38–39, 59–60;
purpose of, 39–41
Book of Mormon: overview
of, xiv, 112–13; stories
of conversion through,
105–6, 116–17; prophecies
concerning, 106–12;
verification of translation of,
110–12
Buddhism and golden rule, 16

C

Calvin, John, on salvation, 55
Celestial kingdom, 124–25
Church of Jesus Christ:
  organization of, 75–78;
  offices in, 76–78; unpaid
  lay ministry of, 78–82; is
  the one true church, 87–88;
  name of, 115
Civil War, Joseph Smith
  prophesies, 102–3
Constantine, 90–91
Coveting, 49–50

D

Dark Ages, 90
Death, 121. *See also* Postmortal
  existence, Spirit world,
  Spiritual death
Degrees of glory, 124–25
Douglas, Stephen A., and
  Joseph Smith, 101–2

E

Ephraim, 107–8
Essenes and baptism by
  immersion, 16
Eve, 25–27

F

Faith: and works, 54–59;
  definition of, 53–54, 56; vs.

belief, 54–58; and prayer
  and fasting, 57
Fall of humanity, 25–27
Fornication, 47–48

G

Genealogy, 131–32
God: is father to human race,
  4–6; has body of flesh and
  bones, 10–14; commands to
  have no other gods, 44–45
Godhead, 7–14; three separate
  beings in, 8–10, 13
Godly sorrow, 62
Gospel of Jesus Christ:
  antiquity of, 15–18; portions
  of, found in other religions,
  15–18; restoration of, 91–93
Grace and salvation, 30, 54–58

H

Harris, Martin, and Book of
  Mormon translation, 110–12
Healing: girl and arrow wound,
  58–59; and priesthood,
  138–39
Hell, 123–25. *See also*
  Judgment, Outer darkness,
  Postmortal existence
Holy Ghost: role of, 7–10,
  71–73; influence of, before
  baptism, 73; obedience to
  promptings of, 72–73

I

Incest, 48
Isaiah: prophesies of modern
  day, 89, 92; prophesies of
  Book of Mormon, 109–10,
  112

J

Jehovah, 20–22
Jesus Christ. *See* Atonement
  of Jesus Christ, Godhead,
  Jehovah, Repentance
Jesus the Christ, 26
Joseph (Old Testament
  prophet), 107–8
Judgment, 123–25

K

Keys, woman's vision of, 3

L

Law of Moses, 43–44
Lazarus, story of, 121–22
Lee, Harold B., on prayer, xvi;
Luther, Martin, on salvation, 55

M

Manasseh, 107–8
Marriage, eternal, 133–35
McConkie, Bruce R., on
  eternal marriage, 135

Ministers, payment of, 78–81
Missionaries, woman sees in
  dream, 105–6
Moral agency, 39, 40–41
Mormons, xiii–xiv
Mortality, purpose of, 26,
  39–41
Mosaic law, 50
Murder, 47

O

Old Testament and Jesus
  Christ, 19–22
Outer darkness, 125

P

Paradise, 129–30
Parents, honoring, 46–47
Patriarchal blessings, 107,
  137–38
Perkins, David Hunter,
  daughter's arrow wound
  healed, 58–59
Philosophies and gospel of
  Jesus Christ, 15–18
Postmortal existence, 121–22,
  124–25; as opportunity to
  accept Christ, 128–32
Prayer: before Senate sessions,
  xv; guide to, xvi–xvii;
  requires faith, 60
Premortal existence, 4–5
Priesthood: importance of, in
  God's plan, 75–76, 84–85;

NOTES

NOTES

NOTES

NOTES

ABOUT THE AUTHOR

Orrin Hatch has been a United States senator (R-Utah) since 1976. He received his juris doctorate in 1962 from the University of Pittsburgh Law School and has been awarded honorary doctorate degrees from ten colleges and universities, including the University of Maryland, Pepperdine University, Southern Utah University, and Samford University.

Noted for his commitment to principles of limited government, tax restraint, and integrity in public service, Senator Hatch has passed legislation covering everything from tough criminal laws to AIDS research, from reducing drug costs to child care. He is most proud of his Religious Freedom Restoration Act, which brought together a coalition of religious faiths from liberal to conservative, and the Religious Liberty Protection Act, which protects religions from untoward political intrusions. He has participated in confirming the appointments of more than 1,000 federal judges, including the majority of the Supreme Court justices over the years. During the Reagan years, he chaired the Health, Education, Labor, and Pensions Senate Committee. As chairman of the Senate Judiciary Committee, Senator Hatch is a leader in the fight for tougher anticrime laws, civil justice reform, and legislation to protect individual property rights. He serves as the current Republican leader and highest-ranking member of the Senate Committee of Finance, the most powerful committee in the Senate.

In addition to his public service, Senator Hatch is a deeply religious man. A member of The Church of Jesus Christ of Latter-day Saints, he has been a high councilman and a bishop and has served a number of missions for the Church, including one full-time mission to Ohio, Indiana, and Michigan.

Senator Hatch and his wife, Elaine, have six children, twenty-three grandchildren, and ten great-grandchildren.

0 26575 11596 3